MW00624334

Closed Legs *DO* Get Fed:
Navigating Celibacy In Today's World

D. Danyelle

All rights reserved. No part of this series of books may be used or reproduced by any means, graphic, electronic or mechanical, including, photocopying, recording, taping or by an information storage retrieval system without the written permission of the author or publisher except in the event of quotes embodied in articles and reviews.
The work is a work of Non-Fiction. The information, statements, facts are presented to the best of the Author's ability with proper citations and acknowledgements.

Copyright © 2013 Kirabaco Publishing. All rights reserved.

The views expressed in this work are solely those of the author and do not necessarily reflect the views of the publisher, and the publisher hereby disclaims any responsibility for them.

Table of Contents

ACKNOWLEDGEMENTS & GRATITUDE

I know that no
man is an island unto himself and my gratitude overflows for those who so willingly inhabit mine with their love, support, and prayers. None of this would be possible without my sustained faith in God, I am eternally grateful that my experiences in my relationship with Him have allowed me to express myself in these written words.

To the matriarch of my island, my publisher, editor, and Mommy: Thank you for your unyielding love and unfailing support. You have always supported me in everything I ever thought to put my hand to do. Thank you for patiently answering a million and one questions and concerns I had not only with writing but also with life! Thank you for instilling in me that my sensuality and sexuality as a woman was nothing to hold shame about. Without that foundation, I would never have been able to write this book. Words always fail me in expressing the love I have for you but thank you for always being my road dawg, my teacher, and my super best friend! Now come on, Singvangelist! We got a tour bus to get on so we can sang down Zion! [inside joke :)]

To my Dad: Thank you for always being ready to step in and fight every battle for me. Your love as a father has always shown me what love I should expect from any man who comes into my life. Our relationship was not always perfect, but I'm thankful we serve a God who mends brokenness. And yes, Dad, I'll give you grandchildren one day!

To my Bonus Dad & Bonus Mom: You have both been incredible spouses to each of my parents after their divorce. Rick, my Bonus Dad, thank you for never being afraid to step in whenever you were needed. Thank you for the love you've shown my mom and the value that you've added to both of our lives. Chevonna, my Bonus Mom, thank you for always being an open ear. You always made yourself available for and to me and went above the call of duty for a stepparent. Thank you both for the love and acceptance you've given to me in our blended families.

To my heart, Mic J: Thank you for your love and support before I ever even put pen to paper. I've been able to rely on your friendship that expects nothing in return for the last eight years of our lives. The two years that I've been able to call you my love have been nothing short of an incredible teaching experience. Your faith and love for God leaves me awestruck and your unquestionable love for me inspires everything that I do. You love me the way that God loves us: unselfishly and in spite of me. Now if you could only get saved LOL! [I'm kidding, I'm kidding. Another inside joke there.]

To JMW & SRS: What would I do without the two of you? This book would have been nearly impossible without you. Thank you for allowing the late night phone calls and book-length text messages whenever I needed you. You have both offered me your homes, your minds, and your shoulders to cry on when the world felt too much to bear. JMW, I'm honored to be your "voice of reason" and hope that this book makes you proud. SRS, you are an amazing woman and I'm honored to be your friend. Ladies, here's to another decade of love, laughter, and unfailing support.

To Jay & Chany: From Charter to Goldie, from Trinama to "Sutter Homes" to Madd Colors, what haven't we been through together? A friendship that has grown to a kinship for over ten years and counting. You all support me in everything I do even if you don't know I'm doing it! Y'all, I know we don't say it often enough because it rarely needs to be said but I love you both infinitely. Jay, thank you for the many nights of AIM Church (which graduated to BBM and iMessage LOL), prayer, and for being my sounding board. Chany, thank you for being the sister God didn't see fit to give me biologically and for often keeping me from eating fruit cocktail off of prison floors (LOL). Though we may go weeks without talking, I know that when we speak we never miss a beat. Love y'all!

To KPI: Honey thank you for your constant transparency and spirit of stewardship. Your humility inspires me and I pray that God continues to show out in your life. Thank you for the countless pieces of advice you've given me both directly and indirectly. You're awesome! To SJP, TCC, & Ru: You all have been some of the most wonderful friends I could have asked for in the last four years. SJP, thank you for always being a listening ear all those days in your office and evenings on GroupMe! Who else would be willing to jump in on my random singing and dancing but you? Ru, thank you for being a wonderful young woman (even in the midst of your random disappearing acts lol) and for your contributions to "the playlist" LOL! TCC, my ride or die crew, thank you for always putting up with my brashness in public and not disowning me LOL!

To Queeny, Jen, (Future Dr.) Lauren, my mentors and professors in AAS, The Alonzo A. Crim Center for Urban Educational Excellence Fam: Thank you, thank you, and thank you! I love y'all!

Even if I haven't singled you out, please charge it to my mind and not my heart. If you have ever encouraged me, loved me, supported me, or even if you didn't: thank you. Your contributions to my life have helped shape who I am and will become.

*This book is dedicated
to every person who has ever questioned
the "because God said so" rationale of sexual
celibacy.
I hope you find your answers within.*

PROLOGUE

Sex is the one thing we love to do but hate to discuss in intimate detail. We enjoy the physical sensations and euphoric high that a great orgasm brings, but we shy away from discussing what sex means for ourselves, our relationships, and the health of our spirit. If you've spent any amount of time in the traditional Christian church, you've probably heard more than one sermon condemning fornication with hellfire and brimstone. It's unlikely however that you've heard *why* God calls us to sexual purity other than "because I said so."

We serve a God who, like any great parent, doesn't instruct us to do something just because He commands it to be so. You've heard the same scriptures over and over again telling you why sex is exclusive to marriage – but in this age where we're completely immersed in sexual behaviors at every turn, it's difficult to understand the relevancy of celibacy to our lives. The hope of this book is to delve beyond not having sex before marriage simply "because God said so," but into understanding what celibacy means, how it profits us spiritually and physically, how to commit to celibacy, and how to be successfully celibate in today's society.

Closed Legs Do Get Fed will not teach you how to use celibacy to manipulate a partner into any specific action such as engagement, marriage, garnering material things, or the like. It will not give you cause to believe that celibacy is a bargaining chip for God to bless your life immediately with a spouse or material gain. This book will not shoulder the responsibility of sexual morality solely on the shoulders of Christian women as we are **all** called to a higher moral standard in Christ. It is, however, my hope that it will give you a solid understanding of the fullness of intimacy and encouragement to boldly address the mysteries of sexuality as a Christian in your life.

Closed Legs Do Get Fed will address sexuality from a heteronormative, Christian view, as this is my primary lived experience. However it is my hope that the ideas, principles, and thoughts in this work apply to those outside of this spectrum – having a responsible sexual life that considers the health of the spirit and the physical body is not exclusive to any religion or orientation.

The words and experiences detailed in *Closed Legs Do Get Fed* are not from those of a perfect person looking down on your imperfections. They are the words of someone who was and is the first partaker of everything you're reading. Not everyone will have feelings of warmth and happiness while they read this book. In fact, some parts may upset and cause you to put this book down. You may finish reading this book and still not choose to live a life of celibacy, at least not within this day or hour or minute; but it is my humble prayer that these words plant the seeds of introspection, reflection, and wisdom within you. In the words of Proverbs 4:5-7 (NLT), *"Get wisdom; develop good judgment. Don't forget my words or turn away from them. Don't turn your back on wisdom, for she will protect you. Love her, and she will guard you. Getting wisdom is the wisest thing you can do!"*

1: I'M NOT 'BOUT THIS CELIBACY LIFE

Celibacy is simply defined as one who is unmarried and does not have sexual relations with another person. Much like eating sugary snacks when attempting to lose weight, we know we shouldn't but we don't completely understand why we shouldn't. Certainly we can have that sugary snack seeing as we're doing everything else right: regular exercise, balanced diet, consistent effort and motivation. So that one little sugary snack, every week and at the same time isn't going to hurt right? Except it does hurt us, slowing down our progress of improving our health. We end up making so many exceptions for our sugary treat that the once in a while indulgence becomes our normal diet and we completely veer off track from our original goal.

So often, we treat sex this way. We know, according to our pastors' sermons, that sex outside of marriage is wrong. Yet, we deceive ourselves by blanketing our willful disobedience with God's grace and forgiveness. We convince ourselves that all the other things we do correctly negate our small, private sin. Let's be clear: God is capable of forgiving each and every one of our sins and casting them into the sea of forgetfulness. The key to this forgiveness is that we "go, and sin no more" (John 8:11 KJV). But how do we even stop falling into the problem if we don't even

1

understand the source? I believe that we often get comfortable in sex outside of marriage because we don't understand what prompts us to have sex in the first place, nor do we understand the enormous power of sex.

Got to give it Up – Why We Should Get Out of Sexual Sin

The question we have to ask ourselves is why we should even stop having premarital sex in the first place. Let's keep it real: sex is wonderful. It feels great, it has a number of proven medical benefits, it is the easiest form of intimacy in a romantic relationship, and ultimately God created it for our pleasure and benefit. You probably even remembered a great sexual moment while reading that last sentence. Consider this, however:

"Flee from sexual immorality. Every other sin a person commits is outside the body, but the sexually immoral person sins against his own body..." (1 Corinthians 6:18-20).

I have no doubt that you've likely heard this scripture before since it's a favorite in many pulpits but I want to look at it in a different way. We're told sex is the only sin that we commit against ourselves. Think about the last person you had sex with. Now consider all of their wonderful qualities. Then consider all of the things you disliked about them. If you were to compare their negative qualities to your own negatives, how many of them are shared? How many of those qualities did you only see in yourself *after* having

2

sex? When we have sex with someone, we become one flesh whether or not we are married to him or her. Sex opens us up to our most vulnerable self and strips us of the guard to the doorway of our spirit. Sex is an act that exchanges more than feelings between the head and the genitals; sex creates an exchange of energy from the soul and spirit that is nearly impossible to break. When we have sex, we virtually pick up the sins of our sexual partners and add them to our own. So now, you don't only have to crucify your own flesh daily – you've gotta crucify other folks' nonsense too because you've created a soul tie with them. *This* is why it is a sin against our own body: we make our own spiritual way hard when we marry the sins of the flesh from another person with our own.

Sex can also blur our visions in our relationships. Sex often makes us forgive and overlook things that should be a red flag to a damaging relationship. Sexual intimacy can cause us to turn a blind eye to her verbal abuse or his inability to be consistent emotional support. In a past relationship, I sexed over my issues instead of talking about them. My partner was unable to be consistently emotionally invested in our relationship. He often failed to listen or hear when I would pour out my heart. Every argument would be soothed by sex, and even though my body was beneath his, my mind would be filled with questions and insecurities. My sexually created soul tie to him, coupled with my emotional investment, caused me to ignore the

3

still quiet voice of my spirit man who cried out in dissatisfaction and unhappiness. I wasted two years of my life giving my sexual energy to someone and hindered my own emotional and spiritual growth. While I can now look back on it and see where I've learned and matured, I can also recognize how being caught in the trap of sexual sin cost me. Maybe you can relate to my experience. How many bad relationships have you stayed in, sexually participated in, and ignored all the red flags that this was not the relationship for you? Be honest with yourself, are the feelings of blindness, regret, and resentment, from those old relationships yet still lingering? If they are, you have to ask yourself, why you would want to commit the exact same action(s) that landed you in that position in the first place.

How do you feel when you're doing something you know is wrong yet you continue to do it? If you're like most people, you feel a deep sense of shame. Shame is born one of two ways: either through the exposure of our guilt to the public, or through the awareness and enlightenment of our guilt to ourselves. Sex, like the other sins that we fight, can leave us with a sense of shame, which places distance between God and us. When we feel distant from God, we allow our hearts to become hardened and become "dead in [our] transgressions" (Ephesians 2:1 NIV), feeling that we are too unforgivable for the state that we are in. The thing about it is, you won't ever become free from the problem that brings you shame if you don't take it to God in the first place. The amazing thing about it is that, according to Colossians 2:13, God made you alive with Christ and forgave all your sins *while you were dead in your sin.* You don't have to have it all together to give it to God; you just need to have a heart to make the choice to give it to Him.

I Know it's Wrong But... — Examining What Sex Means to You

Having all the rationale in the world as to why you should remove sexual intimacy from your romantic, unmarried relationships will not matter unless and until you examine what sex means to you. If you think honestly and hard enough, you can probably trace the root cause of why you can't seem to let this particular sin go. What unhealed emotions from past and present relationships might sex cover up for you? Are you having sex as an act of rebellion without consideration for the harm it brings to self?

In my previous sexual relationships, sex meant sealing the love and emotional investments made within the emotional relationship. While I was well aware that sex didn't equate love, I felt that if I was in love and believed that my mate was also sufficiently in love with me, it was okay to seal that love with sex. While I can count on one hand the number of sexual partners I've had in a lifetime, the one commonality I realize is that I was afraid to be vulnerable in my sexual relationships. I would never fully let down my guard emotionally during sex or within the context of the relationship. Even though I was sharing and creating sexual energy with them, I never felt safe enough to fully give myself to the relationships because I feared getting hurt. Yet, sex still meant that the relationship should have a sense of permanency — somewhere inside of myself I felt that if a man slept with me that he should be committed to me emotionally, spiritually, and physically. If I'm transparent, I used sex to demonstrate and demand an emotional commitment I was, in reality, unwilling to give. It is not by coincidence that the first time I've been able to fully give myself emotionally is in my current celibate relationship with my significant other. Sex had to be removed from my romantic relationships to understand what role it *should* play as opposed to the role it *does* play.

This is not to say that sex is inextricable from some complex problem of life, many of us have sex simply because we enjoy it and have failed to see how this act of disobedience affects the function of our lives; especially if we feel that we're "getting by and surviving" in the areas that matter most such as health, family, and finances. But if you're reading these words and you truly have a desire to begin or continue to live a life of celibacy, you've got to examine what sex means to you in order to understand what it is that you need to bring under the submission and authority of God. This simply means you have to understand what **you** can control and what **only God** can control and change through prayer and total surrender of the problem to Him. For instance, if you're not big into casual sex then you may find it easy to abstain from sex in the absence of a committed relationship. On the other hand if you know that the lines of love and what it means to express love and intimacy in a relationship is where you typically fall into sexual sin, *this* is an issue that can only be fixed by totally surrendering it to the authority of God. You don't have to wonder, I promise that God is able to keep you from falling (Jude 1:24-25 NLT). Yes, even with the issue of sex!

Celibacy, like any covenant with God, is not to be entered into lightly. And some of you reading this simply aren't ready for this life. Not only will you have to discover what sex means to you, but also you have to fully understand what celibacy will *not* do for you in this journey.

2: CHECK YOUR EXPECTATIONS AT THE DOOR

I know you're reading this, but you just might not be ready for celibacy. I also know this is probably shocking considering the whole premise of this book is to help you embrace and navigate celibacy. However, I don't believe in advising people to jump into Holy Covenants without building a sure foundation; one that is comprised of soul-searching and assuring that your choice of covenant is God-led and not self-absorbed. "But **all** things should be done decently and in order" (1 Corinthians 14:40), and this includes inspecting your expectations for the choice you are undertaking in celibacy.

The following five expectations of what celibacy will do for your life, although common, are all clear indicators that you are not ready for a life of celibacy. If you find that you relate to one or more of these expectations, don't feel defeated. They are not impossible to change; you simply need to know *how* to pray so that the Holy Spirit can be your partner in transforming your mindset.

1. You think being celibate will manipulate the hand of God.

Celibacy is not a bargaining chip you pick up to move the hand of God to bless your life in a material way. You should not expect that simply because you've chosen to be obedient to God in your sex life that you're now fully entitled to be blessed beyond measure—particularly if celibacy is the only change you make while ignoring the other spiritual conflicts in your life. It's simply not true, not by the words of the scripture or by the nature of God. To be completely honest with you, God honors your obedience but when we confess salvation, we are to be holy merely because "He who called you is holy" (1 Peter 1:15).

If you want to be sure that your decision of celibacy is God led, examine your motives for making this choice. Let's say you struggle not only with sexual sin, but also with lying and gossiping. Overall, your greatest struggle may be your finances, an area the overwhelming majority of us want God to bless us in. If you decide in your mind "Well, since I want God to bless my money, I'm going to stop having sex" while ignoring your spiritual weakness of lying and gossiping, you're using this covenant as a bargaining chip to move the hand of God. We can't pick one sin, determine it to be the "biggest" or most heinous of our sins, and then decide that because we give it up that God should honor it by blessing us in the way we desire. Don't get mad at me for saying this, get mad with the word of God:

"People who conceal their sins will not prosper, but if they confess and turn from them, they will receive mercy." (Proverbs 28:13 NLT).

On the other hand, if the intent of your decision to enter a life of celibacy because you know that turning over this spiritual weakness is the only way to overcome your other areas of spiritual struggle then you're on the right path. If you decide in your mind "Lord, I feel that celibacy will be the only way I gain spiritual discernment and patience in my relationships," you've acknowledged in that one statement three spiritual weaknesses (sex, discernment, and patience) that can only be delivered by giving it wholly over to God. This kind of attitude is not one of hoping to manipulate God. It is the kind of heart that God wants from us, a heart that says "God I'm giving you my biggest struggle and the struggles that have been developed as a result of it so that you will bless me with the deliverance that will break these chains in my life."

I'm going to keep it real with you: there have been many times in my relationship with my significant other than I felt that we deserved God's favor because we were honoring Him through sexual celibacy. I often wondered why it was that we struggled through financial and emotional issues when we were doing it the right way! I felt like God was being unfair and unjust, and I'm mature enough to admit that now. What I failed to understand is that we struggled because of the sin of not believing fully in the promises of God and weakened faith and until we fixed *those* problems, we would not reap the full harvest of God.

If you're seeking to move the hand of God, then the first thing you need to pray that God increases in you is your **faith**. FAITH is the only thing that moves the hand of God. If your faith is weak, celibacy alone will not fix that – especially if your expectation is that absence of sexual sin is the golden ticket to Easy Street in your spiritual life. When we reject the promises of God due to our weak faith, the bible tells us that it is a sin that turns our heart away from the living God (Hebrews 3:12 NIV). The only way you will build your faith is to first seek His face and not His hand, draw near to Him, and absorb the mighty promises of God. God has promised to supply all of your needs according to His riches that we've inherited in Christ (Philippians 4:19) – not by attempting to con God by giving up one sin only to replace it with another.

2. You think celibacy means you're going to receive your spouse immediately.

Receiving your God-sent spouse may be delayed by premarital sex, but it also isn't hastened by celibacy. If your focus is not on *being* a worthy spouse instead of *finding* a worthy spouse, you've missed the purpose of singleness from a Christian perspective. We have to understand that marriage is, like all other earthly things of this life, temporary and cannot be carried into death. This wakeup call is brought to you by Matthew 22:30:

"For when the dead rise, they will neither marry nor be given in marriage. In this respect they will be like the angels in heaven."

God wants our focus to be on things that are eternal, things that profit and mature our spiritual self. If The Word tells us that marriage is only temporary, why would we believe that courtship and entering marriage should be the sole focus of our life? God honors marriage and delights in our obedience to him in marriage – but he is not pleased when it takes precedence over our relationship with Him.

If we are not careful, our pursuit of marriage and family can push us right into the sin of idolatry. If you have placed the goal of getting married before the development of your relationship with God, you've fallen into sin. NOTHING should come before our relationship with Christ, period. God has shown time and again those that He used in a mighty way were unmarried. One happens to immediately come to mind – the redeemer that lives within each of us! As far as we know from the Bible, Jesus never took a wife, yet God used him to make the ultimate sacrifice. You are not worthless or worth less to God simply because you're single.

So what is the purpose of being single? Well first I need to explain the purpose of marriage. A dear newlywed friend of mine (who also practiced celibacy with her now husband during their courtship) once told me "marriage

12

and relationships are not for our happiness but for HIS holiness in our lives." Marriage, and relationships that are leading to marriage, will bring to the surface the worst of your internal dysfunction in order to set fire to, and destroy, the things that keep us from drawing near to God. That's not to say that your relationship/marriage will be nothing but trouble, but we should always bear in mind that whatever we put God at the head and helm of will be used for HIS glory. This means it won't always be easy and the time in which you are single is a time to prepare your mind to accept what marriage will mean for your life.

Be honest with yourself: you have some flaws that keep you from being fully ready to enter into marriage. God doesn't call us when we are perfect but he perfects us when we are called. Yet, some of us fail to understand that our singleness is God's call to perfect us for the ministry we are entering into when we marry. While we are single, God expects us to carry out His purpose and plan for our lives in all the things He has called us to do. This desire to do the will of God should be your motivation to celibacy, not because you think you can hoodwink God into doing your will over His perfecting will.

3. You think celibacy is a tool to manipulate your mate.

Three date rule, ninety-day rule, and act like one gender while mimicking another. These are a few of the crazy tips and advice we get for navigating the dating scene these days. They each come with the promises of how seriously a mate will take you, how likely they are to marry you, and what you can get out of the relationship if you follow these convoluted rules. In reality, they're all tools to manipulate our mates into doing what we want instead of "trusting the process" by allowing our relationships to take a natural course with both individuals making a conscious choice about the path of the relationship.

Celibacy in our relationships *should* be used as a way to develop a healthy courtship that is unencumbered by the feelings that sex adds to the relationship. Sex should not be viewed as the ultimate prize or goal within a relationship. This not only cheapens the value of sex but of **you**. I've always hated the notion that virginity is the sole factor that makes a woman (or man, but typically this is slanted more toward women) highly prized. While remaining abstinent until marriage is commendable and remarkable, the shame we tend to heap on those who haven't is crazy! I'm here to remind you that to God you are worth so much more than what lies between your legs. This is why He wants to prepare you so that the prizes your spouse gains are the virtuous person that you are in mind, heart, and spirit. Good sex is merely the expression of a love that has been born and matured within a relationship of two clear-

14

headed individuals who have entered the covenant of marriage.

Believing that the prize is in sex creates an unhealthy relationship and rationale with our choice of celibacy. When we believe that our "body count" (number of sexual partners) entitles us to a spouse more than someone whose count outnumbers our own, we're in this celibacy covenant for the wrong reason. When we believe that celibacy, as an ultimatum to a mate will force them to marry us, we're in our celibacy covenant for the wrong reason. We must always bear in mind that our ultimate goal is to please God through our obedience, not to strip our mate of their God-given freewill through manipulation.

4. You are unable to have an honest conversation about your sexual nature.

Assume that you are currently considering entering into a covenant of celibacy. Now think about all the sexual issues you have that you need to give over to God. Can you be open and completely blunt about these issues without feeling shame or guilt? In order to be accurately prepared for this transition, you have to first lay it all at the feet of the Father. Shame and guilt can, and does, often keep us from being totally transparent with God. Though He is aware of all that afflicts us, He still wants us to admit it to Him.

Do you remember the story of the blind man Bartimaeus who wanted Jesus to heal him? Well, Bartimaeus was sitting on the side of the road when he heard that Jesus was coming. He begged for the savior's mercy even while others were yelling at him to be quiet. Even in the midst of all that chaos, Jesus still heard him and sent for him to come unto Him. Jesus didn't mince words; He point blank asked the man "what do you want me to do for you?" (Mark 10:51 NLT). Like Bartimaeus we assume because God is all knowing, we shouldn't have to verbalize everything that we want. Nevertheless when we really want deliverance and healing, we have to be as bold as Bartimaeus and tell Jesus what we need. Bartimaeus wasn't concerned that he was a beggar or that others around him deemed him unworthy of being touched by The Healer.

Far too often, we let the appearance and evidence of our sexual sin to others keep us from seeking deliverance we desire internally. We let others tell us that because we have children, we ought to "be quiet" instead of asking Jesus to transform and renew our mind from premarital sex. We let others tell us that our sex life has been far too wild, too ongoing, and too sinful to turn it over to God now. If you're unable to move past the opinions of others and cry out in earnest about the issues that afflict you, you are not ready for celibacy. If you can't move past the opinions of others *while* you're having sex in order to seek your deliverance, you surely can't withstand the onslaught of opinions and ridicule that will come with your choice to *no longer* have sex! One of my favorite bible verses is Galatians 1:10 NLT. In fact I love it so much that I have it tattooed on my inner wrist as a daily reminder of my purpose in life. If discussing who and where you are in your sexual nature is a struggle for you due to the opinions of others, meditate on these words:

"Obviously, I'm not trying to win the approval of people, but of God. If pleasing people were my goal, I would not be Christ's servant."

5. You are not ready to be held accountable for the covenant you're creating with God.

One of the easiest ways my SO (significant other) and I are held accountable in our celibacy is to tell others that we are celibate. Even people who share our faith often meet us with raised eyebrows. Still, there are those who live out the word in 1 Thessalonians 5:11, encouraging and building us up to stay the course by holding us accountable to the covenant we've made. Of course there's the not-so-easy accountability we are held to by God in private. Consider this:

"And no creature is hidden from his sight, but all are naked and exposed to the eyes of him to whom we must give account" (Hebrews 4:13 ESV).

The most difficult times of accountability for me are in those moments when we are alone,

17

out of the watchful eye of friends and family who hold us to our words of celibacy covenants. Those moments when the thoughts of "well, just this once wouldn't hurt" or "well, if we just do everything but" cross my mind are when I have to be reminded that my choice to remain celibate until marriage is an act of obedience in order to fulfill my destiny mapped out by God. I would be a bold faced liar if I didn't tell you that there are times my SO and I have had moments of intense sexual tension that almost completely derailed us from the course! But beyond considering what we would sacrifice for those few moments of pleasure, I had to consider that I would have to account to God for the act of disobedience and breaking our covenant.

If you're not in a place where you're ready to place the will of God over your hormones, you're not ready for celibacy. This covenant isn't designed to place you in a cycle of ungodly perfectionism—attempting to attain perfection through self-depreciation and buying into a restrictive system of do's and don'ts that are neither spiritually healthy nor sound—but to move you into a place where your walk with God is deepened and your romantic relationships with others are not blotted by the complications that sex brings. When you make this choice, you *will* be held accountable. People *will* scrutinize what you do and may even be waiting to see you fail! You simply have to understand that God's accountability is for your edification to bring Him glory and move you closer to Him. Simply put, everything we do is about God and we can do nothing apart from Him and perhaps this is the very first thing we must accept before we can move forward in His plans for our lives.

Of course, I don't want to discourage you from celibacy. I only want to discourage you from entering what will be one of the hardest decisions of your life with terrible intentions. Only by making this choice with your eyes wide-open can you reap the full rewards that celibacy brings. Trust me: the reward levels to this are more than you can imagine, touching your life in ways you've probably never considered. Keep in mind that, to whom much is given, much is required in return (Luke 12:48 NLT). If you're not ready for all that celibacy requires then you're not quite ready for the rewards that are given!

3: WHEN TWO BECOME ONE

In chapter one, I described a bit about why we should get out of sexual sin due to the creation of soul ties. It's a concept you may have heard quite a bit about, but not understand as well as you should. Are all soul ties bad? Do they all lead to emotional instability and spiritual desolation? The short answer is absolutely not, but we do need to explore the ones that are detrimental and what causes them.

A soul tie, in its simplest understanding, is an act that draws and binds two souls together spiritually and is symptomatic of an emotional bond that unites us with another person. It is what causes us to be drawn so closely to our faith, friends, and partners. Of course, we understand the positive soul tie created by marriage as ordained by God in Ephesians 5:31 where a man leaves his parents and becomes joined to his wife as one flesh. This soul tie allows a married couple to daily build a healthy and emotionally intimate relationship.

However, bad soul ties can cause us to be drawn like a moth to a flame to people our better judgment would normally tell us to run from. They are what make us stay in emotionally, verbally, and physically abusive relationships. Soul ties are the way that we are manipulated, controlled, and deceived by others we are intimate

20

with. The soul tie becomes the lifeline that we pass our spiritual toxins back and forth through in premature sexual relationships. Soul ties are not just created by sex but also through friendships, and vows, or oaths that we may take.

The Biblical text is pretty clear that we become one with anyone we have sex with: "Don't you realize that if a man joins himself to a prostitute he becomes one body with her? For the scriptures say, 'The two are united into one'" (1 Corinthians 6:16 NLT). Are you having sex with a liar? Then you've become prone to lying. Are you having sex with someone who is envious, manipulative, or lazy? You too become prone to that spiritual trash when you have sex with them. Soul ties, both good and bad, are what cause us to grieve so deeply over the loss of our mates. It doesn't work in the converse that you receive their *positive* qualities through sex, either! When you've created an ungodly soul tie, you can only expect to be transmitted the most ungodly flaws within your sexual partner. When you don't take time to repair the soul damage caused by these ties, you simply continue to become more broken from relationship to relationship and only find it harder to establish permanence because you've given so much of yourself without bothering to repair or replace the damaged parts.

Close friends can also create ungodly soul ties. Have you ever had a close friend that you know without a doubt is toxic to your life but you can't seem to cut them off? Despite how much negativity they add to your life, you find yourself continuing to invite them into the most sensitive areas of your life? That's a destructive soul tie. This type of soul tie is one that we often miss because we become so focused on those that are sexually created. This type of soul tie can even be formed through idolatry of public figures, music, or anything! We can (and do) idolize so many different things that take precedence over our relationship with God—and you can be sure this has created an ungodly soul tie.

If you already know that the vow of marriage binds two souls, you should also know that any other vow also binds our souls to those commitments and oaths. Numbers 30:2 NLT says that if we make a vow to the Lord or swear to an oath that binds us, we should not break our word and will do everything that we have vowed and agreed to do. Have you made any vows or commitments to a project, person, or entity that has bound your soul in a spiritually negative way? You have created an ungodly soul tie. The key here is discerning how that vow has affected your life. This is certainly not a loophole to break vows and oaths that are otherwise not negatively impacting your walk with God!

There are varying ways in which we will experience the emotions birthed through ungodly soul ties. These kinds of soul ties are rarely accompanied by positive feelings and often leave us feeling empty beyond repair. You may feel perplexed, miserable, and distanced from God. Though God is not the author of confusion, but of peace (1 Corinthians 14:33 KJV), we will feel and experience nothing but confusion and illusion in our relationships that have been formed outside of the will of God. When your soul tie is good, you will have peace in your mind and heart about it. However, ungodly soul ties will leave you in conflict of what your emotions say, versus what your spirit man is telling you. You'll continue to feel confusion, know something is off in your relationship, but inexplicably stay with your partner. I'm here to tell you that the explanation isn't all that complicated: you've created a soul tie though the emotional bond you forged with your mate.

Then from all that confusion and conflict, misery is born that cloaks you like a shadow. When your spirit wants to do what is right but your flesh says no, you won't ever find peace! Your days become anxious and filled with sadness, sorrow, and fear. All of these factors come together to strip us of our power to change the situation and further disturbs our restless minds. Our minds rehearse every bad decision we've made which then affects how we feel about the world around us and ourselves. The war that rages within us becomes the battle that we fight with those around us; we begin to project our misery on others around us and seem to have the inability to operate any of our close friend/kinships in order!

Then it all comes together to fulfill the ultimate goal: distancing you from God. In our perplexity, misery, and torment we lose sight of our faith. That soul tie causes us to believe that we

23

ourselves are capable of healing ourselves.
Imagine that: you in all of your confusion really
think you're able to *draw* yourself out of your
confusion! If you've been experiencing these
emotions in an intimate relationship or covenant,
know that you have one or more ungodly soul ties
in your life. Don't fret, however, because there is a
way to sever the ties that bind!

To begin our process of severance, we must
first remove all acts of disobedience from our life.
Whether your disobedience is premarital sex, fake
and toxic friends, or really detrimental sworn
oaths, you've got to get it out of your life for God
to move you beyond your current state. Don't
expect this to be a comfortable process as obeying
God rarely is comfortable. This is a time where
you will conform your plan to God's plan, not His
plan to your comfort! If your soul tie was created
by a vow, you must also sever that through
repentance. Have you ever told a man or woman
that your body was theirs? Maybe you've told
someone you would always be there for them, no
matter what. Sometimes, "what" becomes a choice
between God's will and your personal desires.
Whatever verbal agreements you've made that
creates unwanted soul ties sever them through
prayer.

While celibacy is a phenomenal way to
begin the process of breaking sexually created
soul ties, it is not the only action you must take.
You will explore more as you read through the
book. Choosing celibacy, however, should be

taken up in prayer, and done with eyes wide open, to the process of becoming celibate!

Reflection Questions for Chapters 1-3

The following questions are presented for the sake of introspection and to guide discourse among couples and friends. You are welcome to continue reading the book without answering— no one is keeping score!

1. During your sexually intimate relationships, what does sex mean to you? Is it an expression of love? Is it a way to communicate intent?
2. Has your personal meaning of sex been understood by your partners?
3. At this point in your life, do you feel that celibacy is a realistic commitment for you? Why or why not?
4. If you're considering celibacy, what are your motivations for doing so? What do you hope to gain from this decision?
5. Do you see yourself in any of the Five False Expectations of Celibacy? Which ones do you feel most accurately fits you? What do you intend to do in order to change your outlook?
6. What, if any, are the ungodly soul ties in your life that need to be severed? In what ways do you feel ungodly soul ties have hindered you?

4: THE MIND GAME

The easiest way to understand what to expect if you make the decision to become celibate is to parallel the experiences to those of fasting from food. Understanding celibacy as a sexual fast for the purposes of mending and healing first your spirit and your relationship with God and then your current or future romantic relationships will help you to digest the expected outcomes of your decision. There are four stages of fasting: preparation, psychological hunger, toxin release, and healing.

1. *Preparing for the fast.* When properly preparing for a fast, one would begin to slowly reduce food intake over the course of a couple weeks. One might give up meat first, followed by pastas and grains, dairy, fruits, vegetables, and nuts until finally all that's left is water to begin the complete fast. This is done generally so the body doesn't go into violent shock by sudden elimination but also to prepare the mind for the task you are about to take on! Beginning celibacy is no different. It begins with a thought and is followed by removal of things that would hinder us from our commitment. Instead of food groups, maybe your hindrances come in the form of:

a.   *Tempting Text Buddies:* Do you have numbers in your phone that you know would be more than willing to give you sex without so much as a second thought? An ex that you're still sexually friendly with or someone who serves no other purpose than a convenient tryst on a lonely night? Then it's time to clean your contacts. This is a crucial step in the housecleaning involved in preparation for celibacy. You'd be amazed how many "I ain't heard from you in a minute, what's up" texts come out of the woodworks when you decide to make a change in your life. You must know what temptations you can and cannot resist. Your initial state of celibacy may be one of your most vulnerable. As such, it's just easier to cut ties and move forward than to leave doors open for your downfall to enter through.

b.   *Indulgent Triggers:* You may find that you have to remove certain indulgences in your life when you begin celibacy. This could include media such as highly sexualized music or television shows. Not because these mediums are sinful in and of themselves, but because they could trigger feelings in you that you cannot overcome and may derail your celibacy covenant. If you have a song that you know makes you want to call someone when you hear it, take it out of your rotation. Watch shows with gratuitous sex scenes that get you going? It's time to take that show of your lineup. You must use your discernment to know what you can handle in this stage of your journey.

2.   *Psychological Hunger.* When fasting from food, the immediate thing you feel is an intense hunger. Many of your thoughts are consumed by food and eating, you have phantom tastes and scents, and your palette seems to be on overdrive! Your mind will tell you that you're hungry beyond reasonable comprehension and it is the stage that many of us fail to pass during fasting. There too is a psychological hunger for sex when we remove it from our lives. You may experience overwhelming thoughts of sex and feelings that tell you that everything would be better if you could "just take the edge off" by having sex. Those who are fasting from food and begin to lose their resolve at this stage will add broths and tea to their diet until the hunger passes. For those of us who are celibate, we too must add to our diet until the hunger passes. Spiritually, we must turn to prayer

and the word of God to shore up our resolve. In the natural, it helps to talk to others who are or have been celibate who can encourage you with the testimonies of their journey. It is important to remember that you aren't doing this alone. The Holy Spirit and supportive friends/family are here as your partners to get through this!

3.   *Toxin Release.* In this stage of fasting, the body begins to release all the toxins that have built up in our body from poor diet and damage. Those who are fasting usually experience fatigue and a coated tongue accompanied by foul breath and body odor. For those of us who become celibate, we too will experience a toxin release of much of our unresolved issues that stinks just as bad! Some of these include:

a.   *Low Self-Esteem:* Low self-esteem goes beyond hindering our relationship with intimate partners. It keeps us from God, which far outweighs the importance of any other relationship in our life. The book of Proverbs tells us in verse 23:7 us that what we think we *is* what we are! Low self-esteem can convince us that we are worthless and out of place both within our circle of community and with God. These feelings will keep us from doing the work God has set before us. So if you're struggling with self-esteem, expect it to surface during your sexual fast!

b.   *Parent/Family Issues*: If you have any sort of resentment or anger with your parents or siblings, you will be forced to confront it during your fasting. Resentment of our closest family members can cause discord in our relationships! If you felt abandoned by a parent or felt that your parent favored another sibling over you, you will tend to have those feelings triggered in relationships if you fail to deal with them. Of course, not everyone has these issues but if you do, don't be surprised when they surface!

c.   *Spiritual Flaws*: The bible is actually quite clear in concisely detailing our common spiritual flaws. If while you've been "following the desires of your sinful nature," you may have picked up the issues of sexual immorality, impurity, lust, idolatry, sorcery, hostility, fighting, jealousy, irrational anger, selfish ambition, dissension, division, envy, drunkenness, wild parties, and other sins like these (Galatians 19-21 NLT). When you begin to fast, you will find that your spiritual growth conflicts with the flaws that your sin has added to you—the two cannot reside in the same space. So definitely expect to be purged of these toxins during your sexual fast.

4.   *Healing*. This stage is the most rewarding yet the hardest to attain. So many of us get sick and give up at the earlier stages because of their exceeding difficulty. How many of us want to intentionally give up our comfort in exchange for discomfort? God is truly able to bring about healing for every toxin you will release during your celibacy! If we see it to completion, we receive the reward of replacing our toxins with the fruits of love, joy, patience, kindness, goodness, faithfulness, gentleness and self-control (Galatians 5:22-23 NLT).

While you may regret breaking a fast before completion, you will never walk away regretting the changes you experience if you see it through to the finish! When we have sex, so often our sexual partners take more away from us than we can replenish. Yet when we replace their presence with the presence of God through celibacy, the gift He gives us replenishes our losses and then some! You may feel that you want to give up or wonder if certain stages of your celibacy will ever end but don't be discouraged! Not only will all stages come to a close if you see it through, you will get to a place of normalization after healing where you are both comfortable and confidant in your covenant. This confidence will carry you through many "meantime" periods of your life and will continue to yield fruit in your life as long as you keep God at the helm and head of your choice!

5: IN THE MEANTIME: WHAT TO EXPECT WHILE SINGLE

Singleness seems to be the bane of our existence these days. Although we millennials are delaying marriage until later in life, we still place a heavy emphasis on being coupled. Our social network feeds are filled to the brim with pictures of our friends with their #Him or #Her and #MeAndBae which serve as stinging reminders of our singlehood—it's enough to make you vomit! The last thing you generally want to hear as a single person is "being single is a blessing! You should appreciate this time in your life!" I hate to be the bearer of bad news, but what I have to say isn't much different.

Being single is a blessed time in your life, in large part because it's the only time in your life where you and your journey are your only concern. Being coupled (especially if you're in a Christ-centered relationship) means you have to put in much more work and concern yourself with your journey, your mate's journey, and your collective journey. However, that's a tale for another chapter. This chapter focuses on the benefits of being saved, sexy, and single; while being celibate and focused on the purpose of your singleness, from an emotional and spiritual perspective.

Instead of loathing being single, let's talk openly about how this period of your life is absolutely awesome. Even if you desire affectionate companionship, being single is a necessary prerequisite to a successful relationship. Yes, you could leave sex in the equation of your singleness but if you've been doing that so far and getting disastrous results, isn't it time to try something new? Let's examine the benefits of being celibate while single!

- *Celibacy during singlehood allows you to embrace your individuality.* Singleness truly allows you to get to know yourself for all of your award-winning qualities and crippling flaws. Time alone allows time for undisturbed introspection, time to really understand everything from what makes us tick to what our life goals for success are and even what we want in our next relationship. If you don't truly know yourself, you don't know what you have to offer to the romantic relationship that you want! When we aren't intimately familiar with ourselves, we tend to demand things of our partners we are incapable of demanding of ourselves, which leads to conflict in our romantic relationships.
- *Celibacy during singlehood allows you to reclaim power of your sexuality.* Sex tends to give us an out to be passively involved in the emotional development of our relationships. Think

about it: in how many of your sexual relationships have you expected that sex should define the intimacy and expectations of the relationship? We typically use sex to tell our partners that we desire a deeper level of intimacy or, worse yet, that we want a long-term monogamous relationship. Choosing celibacy during your singleness will equip you with the tools to force real, open **conversations** with your mate to decide what your relationship looks like. This will allow you to reserve your sexual energy for your future spouse only to communicate the shared love you've built and for *your* physical and sacred pleasure— THAT'S IT!

- *Celibacy during singlehood will strengthen you emotionally.* How many times have you had sex to escape feeling sad, stressed, or any other feeling in-between? So often sex becomes our indulgence to avoid dealing with our inner turmoil, but we end up with more problems than we started with, when that sex is with someone who has just as many unresolved issue as we do! Of course, there is the possibility that you will find another unhealthy coping mechanism. Being saved doesn't exclude us from the chemical makeup of our bodies or the facts of psychology. If you find it difficult to face your negative feelings head on even with prayer, never be ashamed to seek professional help. The hope is, however, that by removing sex, you are forced to actually deal with these feelings as they arise which will embolden your emotional state.

• *Celibacy during singlehood may provide physical benefits.* While you are celibate, you may experience a rush of mental clarity and physical energy. Understanding celibacy as a sexual fast, fasts are known to provide mental and spiritual clarity after the initial detoxification phase. You may find energy for more physical activities such as working out or outdoor activities since you'll have to release that pent up sexual frustration somewhere! Not to mention, you don't have to worry about contracting a sexually transmitted infection or pregnancy. Though it is worth noting that if you've ever been sexually active, you should still be regularly testing for HIV even during celibacy. HIV-infected cells can hide from your immune system and lie dormant for months or even years.[1]

• *Celibacy during singlehood allows you to live your life for you alone.*

---

[1] U.S. Department of Health and Human Services, National Institutes of Health. (2013). *HIV hides from the immune system.* Retrieved from National Institutes of Health website: http://www.niaid.nih.gov/topics/HIVAIDS/Understanding/B iology/pages/hidesimmunesystem.aspx

• Assuming you are also childless, being single and celibate means you have nothing to hold you back! You can take that dream job that requires long hours without concerns of how it will affect a partner or child. You can travel on a dime, you can move and start a new life wherever your dreams take you, and the only person you have to account to and for is yourself. Now of course, you could do all of these things while single and having sex; but if you're single and have a "friend with benefits" (someone with whom you have sex but are not in a committed relationship with), what issues may arise if and when you try to sever those ties? Regardless to your level of commitment, energy is exchanged during sex that makes cutting ties a little more difficult than usual. As we've already discovered, sex invites many new layers of issues to otherwise simple situations. Choosing celibacy during singleness cuts away all the sex-related drama and allows you to be as self-focused as you wish.

• *Celibacy during singlehood allows for dating without pressure.* When you choose to accept a date from a potential partner, celibacy will help you rest assured that you do not have to deal with the awkwardness of the sex game. I don't mean just avoiding running the risk of a bland sex experience from one-night or three-date stand. Celibacy removes the mental negotiation about sex and gives you a chance to just enjoy your date without wondering "what will they think if I have sex after this date?" Remember, we choose celibacy to strengthen our ministry and purpose in God, not to escape adding a person to the arbitrary body count and avoid being labeled as whore or slut. Your body count, whether high or low, should never be the basis of what you have to offer to a relationship as a complimentary mate. Who you are in spirit, mind, and heart should be chief among what you bring to the relationship table.

Celibacy has overwhelming benefits but you must understand that removing sex from our romantic relationships doesn't mean that we strive to eradicate your sensual and sexual nature forever. Our goal is to approach sex in a healthy way and engage in it with the spiritual and emotional maturity that God designed for us.

I'm Single but My Issues Aren't: Three Areas of Emotional Healing

We may not know how long our period of singleness is, but we can be assured that it is a great time to deal with ourselves in spirit and in truth. There are at least three emotional areas in which you may need to deal, heal, and move on from before you're ready to be in a relationship.

1. Emotional Baggage

"*Ugh, I can't stand all men/women. Ain't none of 'em no good!*" Emotional baggage is one of the biggest reasons we can't successfully move out—and stay out—of singlehood. We picked up the baggage of neglect and misuse from our first relationship, and carried it into our next relationship, before picking up baggage of unhealthy mindsets, and carrying it into the next relationship. We begin to carry entire luggage sets from relationship to relationship, developing crippled defenses and a deep sense of hatred for our partners past and present. Sure, all well-adjusted and well-lived people have baggage and none of us is exempt. Yet when your baggage blinds you from the role you played in packing it, you have a problem.

You should also consider the family baggage. Maybe you have been making poor relationship choices because you've only seen poor relationships modeled before you. What kind of relationships did you grow up seeing your parent(s) having? What about older siblings, or aunts and uncles? We model our expectations from the behaviors of those who have the responsibility of teaching us many of our foundational concepts—our family. Ask yourself what baggage you've carried from your childhood into your adult intimate relationships. Has it all been good or is it the root cause for some of your emotional immaturity?

Ultimately, the common denominator in your failed relationships is **you.** That may sound harsh, but you have to realize that it is our unresolved emotional issues that cause us to pick mates who have the same characteristics, that cause us pain and disappointment. It's not that all men/women are no good, it's that your emotional state as it concerns relationships is no good. Even if a good person comes along, if you're punishing them for the mistakes and errors of past relationships, they won't be around for long. Celibacy alone will not heal you from this blindness if you insist on being in denial that it exists. Spend some time unpacking your luggage so you can go into your next relationship with your best emotional self that is open, and ready, to love.

2. Fear of Intimacy

Fear of being close or emotionally attached to another person is not a healthy mindset to enter celibacy with. Love is work and being emotionally vulnerable is one of the greatest risks we take in life. If you've been incredibly disappointed in past intimate relationships, you may have unwittingly developed a fear of emotional attachments. If this is you, "I'll never let another person hurt me like that again," just might be your personal pledge of allegiance. People who fear intimacy want others around but never want them to get too close for comfort. This person, realizing that there is no more intimate act than sex between two people, may cleave to celibacy as a method to avoid emotional investment within interpersonal relationships. This is *totally* unhealthy and should be dealt with before entering into a celibacy covenant. While you're single, take some time to put the focus on the situation that caused you to build an emotional dam. Remember that above all the feelings of hurt and disappointment you have survived up to this point. Your survival is an indication that God has a greater plan. It's time to dismantle the dam!

3. Unresolved Sexual Trauma

If you have been sexually assaulted, abused, or raped then you likely have a very complex attitude toward, and emotional concept of, sex. This is one instance wherein it is completely understandable to have a fear of intimacy. However, it is for our benefit that we deal, and heal even from, such a traumatic experience. Choosing celibacy *with* unresolved sexual trauma *without* intentions to resolve it is harmful because the core issue remains unaddressed. If you have been sexually traumatized and recognize that it must be dealt with and have chosen celibacy as a result, that is a great mindset to enter into celibacy with.

Sexual trauma tends to bring with it shame, depression, and fear of intimacy—all of which are things that will hinder our spiritual maturity and ministry. It would be irresponsible of me to tell you to *only* pray about unresolved sexual trauma. That doesn't speak to the very real anger and disappointment you may have with God. You might be asking, "Where was God when I was molested, assaulted, abused, and/or raped? Especially by someone I trusted?" The only answer I have for you is that while the person to whom God entrusted to care for you chose to do such a despicable and evil act, God is still in the business of healing. Sometimes, God's answer to our healing is through professional counseling services such as a therapist or psychologist. The Holy Spirit will partner with you for your healing in showing you *how* to pray; such as prayers that God bring the unresolved issues to the surface and help you realize that they need healing and resolution. A therapist or psychologist can be a partner in the natural to give professional and educated assistance of ways to cope and work through the trauma of this experience. Only after you have closure and resolution to this issue should you commit to celibacy.

Still think singlehood serves no purpose? Imagine trying to grapple with the aforementioned issues while in a relationship where you're responsible for the proper care and love of someone else's heart and feelings. God gives us a period of singleness to be of better service to ourselves and to others. Singleness prepares you for the pressure cooker that will be your decision to become and remain celibate. Your celibacy walk is going to require a deeper prayer life, spiritual introspection, and emotional inventory of your life stock! Treasure your time as a single person to seek God's face without intrusion or distraction from the obligations that come with relationships, marriage, and family.

Reflection Questions for Chapters 4 & 5

The following questions are presented for the sake of introspection and to guide discourse among couples and friends. You are welcome to continue reading the book without answering— no one is keeping score!

1.   If you've ever tried celibacy before, did you experience the stages as described in *Chapter 4: The Mind Game?*

2.   What stage, if any, do you get stuck at during your celibacy fast? Why do you feel that you cannot get beyond this stage?

3.   If you're single, what benefits as described in Chapter 5 are you most excited to gain during celibacy? Are there any that you fear or feel like won't be as beneficial for you?

4.   If you're currently single (not dating or in a relationship) and having sex, do you feel sex has kept you from a committed relationship?

5.   Do you see yourself in any of the three areas of emotional healing in Chapter 5?

6: I MET SOMEONE: CONVERSATIONS OF CELIBACY AND MONOGAMY

Score! You've met someone and after a time of dating, you are sure that you're ready to check out of Singleness Inn & Suites. You've spent time getting to know yourself as an individual, you're sure of what you have to offer, and you know what you're looking for out of a relationship. You've made a commitment to celibacy and have all intentions of sticking to it, but now you've got to figure out how this decision affects someone outside of you. Up to this point, your decision of celibacy only affected your life but when making the decision to enter into a relationship with someone, you have to consider how his or her life will considerably change! What if the person you want to date is not celibate and, as far as you know, has no intentions to be? How do you broach the conversation of celibacy in a way that expresses where you are spiritually without alienating your potential new mate? I'm so glad you asked.

The first question you have to ask yourself is if you're really headed toward a monogamous relationship. This may seem like a captain obvious point, but the reality is in this day and age we operate relationships based off assumption. Oh, you've heard of and witnessed those relationships that don't operate with titles because "titles don't mean anything, we got an understanding." Let me tell you something: the only understanding you will have in an untitled relationship, when you want a title, is an understanding of being pissed off. Giving the benefit of the doubt here, there are people for whom untitled relationships work. Titles, however, give clear parameters to the relationship and establish a standard to which its participants must be accountable. THAT is the key here! How much loyalty do you owe someone who takes your feelings on the basis of an "understanding" knowing that you want a full blown committed relationship? What disservice do you do to yourself accepting such an arrangement? In my current relationship, my SO (significant other) was very deliberate about the titles he would use to introduce me to his family, friends, and associates. We knew each other seven years prior to us beginning the process of dating and courtship! When we started getting closer as friends, he introduced me as his friend. As our friendship blossomed into dating, he introduced me as his lady friend that he was dating. When we entered an exclusive, monogamous, and committed relationship, he introduced me as his girlfriend and other affectionate nicknames. At the onset of our relationship, however, I made it clear what I wanted and a simple "understanding" without the boundaries and accountability that titles bring, was not among my interests. So before you begin the conversation on celibacy, you need to be certain that your conversation is with someone you're in a relationship with.

You may wonder if withholding your celibacy decision during the early dating phase is deceptive. On one hand, you could tell someone on a first date that you're celibate to cut out the nonsense if that person isn't interested in a long-term relationship. Do consider that you could be using your celibacy as a defense against getting into futile relationships (one that doesn't end in marriage). Dating is useful, in that it teaches us what we do and don't want in a mate, so try not to act in such haste to find *the one* simply because you want to get married and have sex! The dating period is an opportunity to screen a potential mate for their qualities. Stating very early on that you're celibate could preclude a potential romance. After one or two dates, a person may not have enough vested interests in you to stick around after your celibacy declaration, even though they may be very well capable of having a celibate relationship. The one exception to this is if you aren't dating towards marriage, and intend to be completely celibate from sex and/or marriage for a lengthy period or lifetime. If you're strictly looking for companionship through dating, you should be very open and honest about this from the onset of your relationship. On the other hand, if you approach it at the time that you've both figured out that your general attraction has grown to an infatuation that could lead to love; your potential mate should have more of a vested interest in you and be more willing to try celibacy. If your period of dating lasts longer than three months, you should also reconsider your timeline of introducing your celibacy decision. Continuing into four, five, or six months of the dating phase without making your potential romantic partner aware that you are, and intend to remain celibate, is deceptive to them and can set you up to be terribly hurt if or when they break things off. So though both methods would take place before agreeing to a monogamous relationship during the dating phase, it's your call as to when you have *the talk*. Ultimately, though, you can't avoid it forever! You should **never** enter a relationship under false pretenses, your potential partner should know you are, and intend to remain, celibate.

The discussion of establishing a relationship is really a two-part discussion that must include your celibacy decision. Just as you deserve to know that you're in a committed relationship, your mate deserves to know what kind of relationship they're walking into. If they are not now, nor have they ever been celibate, a sudden celibate relationship may be too much for them to realistically handle. The question I get most often when people find out I'm in a celibate relationship is *how* you approach that conversation with a partner. Well, I can tell you that a sure fire way to fail the conversation is to go over the top with the spiritual side. I'm not saying your relationship with God needs to be closeted, not by a long shot. However, if you start off the conversation speaking in tongues and trying to lay hands with anointed oil in the middle of dinner your conversation isn't going to end well. We are spiritual beings having a natural experience which means that even in dealing with matters of the spirit, we have to express it in such a way that it meets others in the place they dwell. Like all conversations, you have to approach the celibacy discussion honestly. Begin by detailing the benefits of celibacy within new relationships:

- *No Reservations at Heartbreak Hotel.* While celibacy doesn't preclude you from all hurt that accompanies romantic relationships, it certainly keeps you from the anger and regret that is born of failed sexual relationships.

- *Learn Unconditional Love.* Celibate relationships often teach us what it means to love someone unconditionally in a romantic sense. If you have children, you've more than likely already learned how to love someone outside of you unconditionally. However, there is a new level of learning to love someone unconditionally in a relationship. Unlike your children or family, you don't share nearly identical upbringings or mutual DNA. Romantic relationships require you learning to love someone who may be completely opposite of you but complimentary in every way. A "lust-ationship," a relationship built purely on sexual lust and attraction, is more likely to fail *if your expectations are that of a relationship that is based on principles of love.* A celibate relationship will allow you to focus on developing an understanding of, and love for, the inner characteristics of your mate.

•   *Breaks the Myth of the Soul Mate.* Celibate relationships will show you just how much work goes into loving someone and maintaining a relationship with them. Removing sex as a tool to passively engage emotionally in your relationships will help you to realize that there is no perfect person waiting around the corner who will fulfill your fantasies. Celibate relationships will strip down your partner expectations to the qualities that truly matter—those that will lend themselves to working the higher purpose of your relationship: HIS holiness!

So at this point in the conversation, you've established why you've chosen celibacy and why you feel like it would be a good look for your relationship. Maybe they're feeling you, maybe they're not. The one thing I find that celibate people tend to do in new relationships is simply state that they are celibate and their new mate can either take it or leave it. While ultimately your new mate really does have the option of getting with your celibacy or getting lost, there is an entire "in-between" dialogue that is lost. A key component of celibacy discussion is establishing what celibacy will look like for your relationship.

50

Not all celibate relationships operate under the same restrictions and usually only share the commonality that there is no sex until marriage or some other designated milestone. Before agreeing to a committed and celibate relationship, you need to establish how it will play out for you and your partner. Assuming that your goal is celibacy until marriage:

- *How long will you wait?* Celibate relationships are more difficult as they age. You may find it easy to be sex free for three months but what if three months turns into three years? Be honest about your personal willpower. Set checkpoints in the relationship where you come together and evaluate if you both believe you're headed toward marriage and if so, determine a timeline for your road toward marriage. Wading in a sea of uncertainty when it comes to the expiration date of your celibate relationship is a Molotov cocktail for conflict and sexual temptation. Having checkpoints and timelines isn't rushing someone towards something they aren't interested in; it is simply another form of accountability to one another for the covenant you are making.

- *How far can we go?* Some celibate couples choose to not engage in any form of physical intimacy. This includes no kissing, no hugging, no cuddling, or any other form of physical affection that can lead to sex. There are

51

others who are okay with kisses, hugs, and other intimate physical affections that do not include sex. Now, it is safe to say that your celibate relationship cannot include an "everything but" attitude. Be honest with yourself, when's the last time someone orally pleased you and it didn't lead to penetrative sex? There are certain lines you simply cannot cross if you have the intent to keep your covenant. But you do need to assess the willpower of each individual and decide what physical affection you *can* handle without feeling tempted to have sex.

Including these points in your celibacy conversation with your mate will more than likely give them a better understand of not only where you stand but where they will stand if they agree to a relationship with you.

The celibacy conversation between my SO and me is one that I remember quite well. At the point of us talking about it, we'd already been in situations that would have been conducive to us having sex. However, we had never (and have never!) been sexually intimate and seeing that we were headed into a committed relationship, he decided that we needed to establish the parameters of sex between us. He told me that he'd never been celibate before and had in fact been quite sexually active in his life up to that point. However, he wanted to make a sacrifice and try to do this *one* thing God's way in his life. He asked would I be okay if we had a celibate relationship and I told him I would, as I'd already been celibate at that point. Although the phrase *try to be* would be revisited during another sex discussion in our relationship, the boundaries of our relationship were clear from the beginning. I knew what he wanted and I knew what I was getting myself into. The conversation allowed me an opportunity to decide if this vow was one that I could live with successfully.

What do you do when you're already in a relationship that has been sexually intimate? You may feel like starting celibacy in an already sexually involved relationship is pointless. This is simply not true! You too can reap the benefits if you choose to make your sexual relationship a celibate one. The conversation doesn't change. You still need to outline why you feel like this is the best choice for you individually and for your relationship as a whole. Maybe you need the clarity that celibacy brings in a relationship because it's time to make some big decisions (breaking up, entering into an engagement) or life transitions such as entering marriage. Simply be honest with yourself and your partner about your decision, how it will affect your relationship, and where the path takes you from here.

There is still the possibility that your potential or current partner is not getting with the program of celibacy. This is a reality of walking in any obedience to God but especially with celibacy. Most want the answer of "what do you do" to be sugarcoated. You would like to hear that there is a compromise between their will and God's will. I hate to break it to you but there is no compromise to be had. If after you've plainly laid out your reasons for celibacy, how it looks for your relationship, and the timelines leading to a greater commitment your partner isn't with it, you have to consider walking away. We cannot and should not put anything before our relationship with God, including our romantic relationship with our partner. If someone is unwilling to walk with you on this journey they are unlikely the person God has for you right now. Consider the words of Matthew 10:22 ESV:

"and you will be hated by all for my name's sake. But the one who endures to the end will be saved."

We have to endure to the end of what God has called us to do for our reward is greater than our temporary pain. You may have to end your relationship and you will certainly experience the hurts accompanied with that. The good thing is that God is a mender of broken hearts. We don't know the whole plan of God. Who knows? Your partner who was once unwilling to commit may, after some distance and time with God, come back around and be ready to walk this journey with you. However, you must be willing to accept it as the will of God if they aren't. Not everyone will see and embrace the benefits and blessings of celibate relationships. These are just the breaks. Still, there's the chance that your current or potential mate sees the blessing in celibate relationships too and is willing to walk alongside you. Now you have to learn how to navigate the twists and turns of a celibate relationship. Buckle up; it's going to be a wild ride.

7: IN THE MEANTIME: WHAT TO EXPECT IN A RELATIONSHIP

You've talked about it, mapped it out, and are now successfully in a celibate relationship with your partner. You thought broaching the conversation was the hardest part—oh how I wish it were! Once you're in a celibate relationship, you not only have to go through developmental stages and milestones as usual but you also have to actually *maintain* your celibacy. This can feel downright impossible as you begin to fall in love with your partner and you are, up until this life point, accustomed to expressing that love sexually.

In my current relationship, my significant other and I were friends for seven years prior to our romantic involvement. I had a crush on him when we first became friends all those years ago and as such was already sexually attracted to him. Fast forward to when our friendship blossomed into romance, that sexual attraction multiplied exponentially. Compound that sexual tension with being in love and it didn't take much for him to arouse me. It only took the right look, smile, touch, or gesture to have me ready to get to it and do it, celibacy covenant be darned. We would have numerous arguments about him doing things that aroused me while adamantly telling me that we couldn't have sex. It took several conversations to revisit our purpose in celibacy, how it looked within our relationship, and our individual ability to withstand the pressure that came with these decisions.

My goal is never to lie to you about how trying this decision will be. I don't care how healthy your relationship with God is: denying your sensuality is hard. However, we have to keep in mind that "Those who belong to Christ Jesus have nailed the passions and desires of their sinful nature to his cross and crucified them there" (Galatians 5:24 NLT). Keep some spare nails handy because you *will* have to nail these desires down repeatedly during the course of your relationship. In order to keep in mind the benefits of celibate relationships, here are a few nails to get you started:

- *Relationships without the focus of relations.* Choosing celibacy will allow you to have a healthier relationship that focuses on the strength of character of your mate rather than their libido. Prematurely turning a romantic relationship into a sexually active relationship can quickly ruin the effort we put into getting to know our mate by switching our primary focus to sex.

- *Somebody loves you, baby.* Keeping your relationship celibate gives you the assurance that if they stick around and work alongside you to build your relationship, they love you for who you are and not your sexual prowess. This is not to say that sexual relationships are loveless, it is simply to say that keeping it sexless will withdraw the invitation to the complications that sex brings.

•   *Spiritual insight to see the path ahead.* Because celibacy will close the door to the complications of sex, it is easier to pray for God's revelation of the purpose of your relationship. Is this a teaching experience alone or is s/he your life mate? You may not meet "the one" as soon as you establish your first celibate relationship. As mentioned before, celibacy is not a tool to manipulate a partner into what we want or think they should be. Celibate relationships do, however, allow us to date with purpose.

When you experience turmoil in your relationship directly related to the sexual tension that love and celibacy will create, you have to have open and honest dialogue that will bring you to one accord. So what do you do outside of focusing on not having sex in your relationship? I believe there are quite a few things we can do that should be done in the course of any successful relationship.

Equip your toolbox. Oftentimes, we mistakenly believe that the principles and roles of spouses magically occur when we sign a marriage certificate witnessed by a pastor. Your skill development of learning how to submit, compromise, and decide what your marital relationship will look like begins during courtship.

If you're in a relationship headed toward engagement/marriage (or hope to be), let's take a look at the tools your celibate relationship should equip you with:

- *Develop a corporate prayer life.* There is power in prayer. It is one thing to intercede on behalf of your mate, but it is another to learn how to pray with them. We make prayer such a private act that we forget the power in coming together in unity to pray for one another and the relationship as a whole. It takes prayer to hold any Christ-centered relationship together, but it surely takes a little extra to hold a celibate relationship together! Building a healthy corporate prayer life now will make it so much easier to carry it into your marriage where, when faced with the trials of that transition, you will surely need it.

- *Submission.* Marriage isn't going to make you up and know the meaning of Ephesians 5:21-25's definition of marital submission. The most fatal theology I hear about this passage of scripture is the erroneous belief that it erases the opinion of women and gives men power to dominate their spouses. Spoiler: it doesn't. Verse 21 plainly states that spouses should submit to one another out of reverence for Christ. Your submission should come because you respect Christ and the order that He has ordained for marriage. The contentious verse 22 does say that wives should submit to their husbands as to the Lord. However, it is followed up with husbands being instructed to **love** their wives just as Christ loved the church and as they love their own bodies. *"No one hates his own body but feeds and cares for it, just as Christ cares for the church"* (Ephesians 5:29 NLT). Submission is simply this: women, we have to submit to our husbands but we are not to be silenced, dominated, or abused by them. Men, you have to submit to Christ as the head and love your wife so intensely that submission for her is not an issue. Spend time during your pre-marital relationship to learn how to submit to your spouse.

- *Build a support system.* Healthy relationships naturally offer companionship but they aren't always conducive to offering support. Be a consistent support and encouragement to your mate. You can do this by being a soft landing place against the harshness of the world, supporting their goals, and through encouragement to deepen a spiritual walk.

Be yourself. The quickest way to end a relationship is to begin it under false pretenses. The best thing you can do is to be yourself at all times: be it good, bad, or otherwise. You should never present a false image of yourself only to ensnare someone into a relationship. It becomes increasingly difficult to keep up that appearance and eventually the truth will always surface. Allow the health of the relationship to bring to surface your flaws and dysfunction so that you can improve as a person.

Be accountable. Find an accountability couple whose relationship is a step ahead of yours and/or who share your values and faith that can hold you accountable while giving you sound counsel. Single friends who possess godly wisdom can also be sound counsel for you in your relationship. The biggest mistake we can make is expecting our partners to play every single role in our life (parent, friend, sibling, *and* mate). We don't need to sacrifice our friends and family to have healthy relationships. In fact, if you can find your necessary accountability within those circles your relationship will be healthier for it! Accountability partners will not only help keep you to your covenant but they can serve as a sounding board to provide you with sound advice in times of conflict within your relationship.

Navigating your celibate relationship will require much trial and error. The outfit of your celibacy relationship is not something you will choose once and be done with it for the duration of your relationship. Like me, you will likely have to revisit what boundaries must be enacted to ensure that you are strong enough to withstand the pressure of your celibacy covenant. The need to reevaluate is not a sign of failure! As with any relationship, you and your partner must define what works best for the two of you in order to be successful, loving, and happy!

Reflection Questions Chapters 6 & 7

The following questions are presented for the sake of introspection and to guide discourse among couples and friends. You are welcome to continue reading the book without answering— no one is keeping score!

1. How comfortable are you with initiating discussion about monogamy and celibate relationships? If you're uncomfortable, what are some of the concerns you have?
2. What are the parameters and boundaries you and your partner are comfortable with in your celibate relationship?
3. What are the "check-in" milestones of your relationship? A huge part of celibacy in relationships is the ability to be honest about your willpower and self-control. Consider setting "check-in" times to assess the state of your relationships and shared celibacy covenant.
4. If you're already in a sexually intimate relationship, what obstacles to you believe you will need to overcome to begin a celibate relationship?
5. Are you prepared to walk away from a romantic partner if they cannot agree to celibacy?
6. Are you comfortable suggesting and developing a corporate prayer life with your partner? If not, why?

7.   Do you feel that the support system in your relationship is strong? Ask your partner how well supported they feel by you. Ask yourself how well do you feel supported by them.

8.   Do you have an accountability partner or partners to keep you and your mate in check concerning your celibacy covenant? If not, do you have someone in mind that can act in this role?

8: DEVELOPING HEALTHY SEXUAL ATTITUDES

It may seem surprising that a book with an emphasis on celibacy takes the time to discuss the development of healthy sexual attitudes, but if you've gotten this far, you should know that this isn't your usual celibacy discussion.

We have been conditioned by both church and society to be quietly obsessed with the act of sex while simultaneously shrouding it in secrecy. Sex sells everything from our toothpaste to our clothes yet we're told that sexually aware women aren't "good women" while oversexed men are stallions and studs. Our pulpits all but personally escort us to hell for the mere thought of premarital sex. We speak circularly about sex frequently but no one wants to truly answer the questions we have in a positive way. We begin to internalize unhealthy views of sex and our sexual self and carry those ideas into our relationships only to pick up more complex issues as a result.

While I've worked hard to demystify celibacy, I believe it is equally important to discuss sex in a candid way. I'm sure if I haven't already come under fire from the traditional theologians, this chapter will surely seal the deal. However, your wholeness in sexual awareness is important to me. Sexual health goes beyond choosing to have sex or abstain. It requires that we address our preoccupation and complex thought processes surrounding this intimate act. In this chapter we will discuss the Bible's stance on the purpose of sex, learning about our sexual self and desires, and how to have an open, honest conversation about sex with your partner in a pre-marital/engaged relationship.

To Enjoy or Not Enjoy:
Understanding God's Design for Sex

One of the foremost questions about sex is what the Bible has to say about it. Is sex meant to be unmemorable and merely used as a tool for procreation among married couples? The only thing we seem to have a majority consensus on is that sex is gift meant exclusively for marriage. Yet, many of us are still trying to reconcile our sensuality with our spiritual walk given the array of theology we've been taught concerning sex.

Genesis 38:6-10 is probably one of the most used Biblical passages to teach the theology of sexual repression. It is the story of Er, Onan, and Tamar. Er was the first son of Judah and married Tamar but because Er was a wicked man, the Lord took his life. As was customary in that time, Judah required that Onan marry his brother's widow. Onan was required by the law to have a child with Tamar in order to produce an heir for his brother. Onan didn't want to father a child that would not be his child, so he used the not-so-reliable pull out method when the two had sex. The Lord wasn't pleased with Onan's actions and decided to take his life as well. From these four verses, an entire theology of sexual repression was built; a theology that preached

65

that sex was purely for procreation and that masturbation was a sin since the act fails to produce a child.

It is this type of teaching that has shaped our own faulty personal theology. It is worth noting that Genesis is the first book of 66 in the bible and if you delve a little deeper, you will learn just how much God wants us to enjoy sex within marriage. First off, let's get clear that the Lord killed Onan because of his selfish disobedience to the law of the times not because sex is solely meant for procreation. God is pretty upfront about the pleasures that marital sex should bring:

"Drink water from your own well—share your love only with your wife. Why spill the water of your springs in the streets, having sex with just anyone? You should reserve it for yourselves. Never share it with strangers. Let your wife be a fountain of blessing for you. Rejoice in the wife of your youth. She is a loving deer, a graceful doe. Let her breasts satisfy you always. May you always be captivated by her love."

Those words were not from an arabesque novel or a book of romantic poetry, it's straight out of the Bible in Proverbs 5:15-19. Why would God divinely inspire Solomon to write such words of beauty and passion if He meant for sex to be yet another mundane, meaningless task on our to-do list of life? It is also worth noting that the burden of sexual monogamy is not placed solely on the shoulders of women. Solomon asked of *men* why they would go out giving all their sexual energy to other people! Too often, churches have taught women that their sexual nature is wrong and that men are idiotic animals incapable of controlling their sexual desires. Our pastors and religious leaders lay the foundation of our complex relationship with sex. This is especially true for women of color wherein we are "by most measures, the most religious group in the world."[2] The Black Church continues to be a community pillar as one of the few institutions built, financed, and controlled by Blacks.[3] Think about the enormous presence of the church and religion over the course of your life and consider the teachings you've received. Unless you've been lucky to have progressive teachers, your attitudes towards sex have likely been negatively influenced to assume that the sexual fall of man is solely the fault of women. Irresponsible theology has left women with the substantial responsibility of chastity, causing nearly irreconcilable internal conflict between our faith and our sexuality. These verses, however, plainly call men to an

---

[2] Gallup Report (1984) Religion in America.

[3] Drake, ST. C. and H. Cayton (1945) Black Metropolis. New York: Schocken. Frazier, E. F. (1974) The Negro Church in America. New York: Schoken. Nelsen, H. M. and Nelsen A.K. (1975) Black Church in the Sixties. Lexington: Univ. Press of Kentucky.

understanding of the prize that is sexual monogamy with their wives while crediting men with the ability of self-control instead of infantilizing their willpower in the face of female sensuality.

Speaking of Solomon, he was divinely inspired to write an entire book about sex. You might remember seeing it as *Song of Solomon* in the Biblical text. Solomon spent verse after verse discussing the taste of his spouse's kiss, the depth of their love, the breasts of his wife, and the beauty of her countenance. Granted it may not be written in the kind of language that gets you hot and bothered but there is no doubt that the Bible has a home that discusses sex both candidly and enthusiastically. God most certainly designed sex for us to enjoy it in *His* ordained time of marriage because He knows everything that comes with sexual energy created out of time within unmarried relationships.

Self-Discovery: Reconciling Faith & Sexual Desire

We know that we are not capable of handling fully the repercussions of pre-marital sex, but expecting to turn off our sensual nature from the time of puberty until marriage is unrealistic. So what are we to do in order to remain obedient to God, while recognizing that we cannot avoid our physiological wiring? Masturbation or self-love is the healthiest option to not only quell our physical desire but to also understand and express our sexual selves. Between churches, our parents, and socialization, many of us have been taught to believe that self-love is wrong. However, I invite you to question why we attempt to moralize (define as a sinful/immoral or acceptable) masturbation in the first place.

Sexual release decreases stress levels with the release of dopamine by the brain. Releasing sexual tension increases our mood while improving and deepening our sleep. For women masturbation can reduce or relieve menstrual cramping while for men repeated blood flow to the genitals improves and maintains the penis' muscle tone. There are also the obvious benefits of preventing pregnancy, absence of sexually transmitted infections, and avoiding the exchange of unwanted sexual energy. Self-love gives us an option of sexual release, while abstaining from sex with others, and as a result allows us to maintain obedience in our celibacy covenant. So when does self-love become self-destructing?

The sin develops in how you choose to use the act. Arousal develops as a result of sexual desire. The question you must address is: Am I experiencing a temporary desire easily satiated by sexual release or am I driven by lust? Lust is not simply sexual desire, it is *evil* sexual desire driven by a sexual arousal from the debasement and objectification of another person. Lust is often fed by pornography, which tends to debase and objectify women. Pornography, when used excessively, opens the doorway to pornography addiction that (among other things) tends to cause disconnect with sexual expectations and reality. When the sexual fantasies are fueled by obsession, violence, harm, and objectifying sexual acts with another person, your self-love has developed into the sin of self-destruction. When the addiction lends itself to a compulsion that takes overtakes your life, keeping you from the things and people that matter most, it is grown from a perfectly fine and normal habit into a sexual sin. If you see yourself in these words, it is time to face and acknowledge your addiction and seek the necessary help to break free.

Although masturbation is a great outlet for sexual energy during celibacy, it can create a slippery slope. It's not necessarily sinful, unless you've fallen into one of the aforementioned patterns of masturbation, but it is still a form of sexual pleasure that can distract from spiritual growth. It is well possible to be celibate without any form of physical sexual release – we do serve a well capable God after all! As I always admonish, you **must** define how your celibacy will look for you. Only you can be honest enough with yourself to know what boundaries you must erect in order to achieve the promises given to us through the obedience of celibacy.

An Intimate Learning Experience

Celibate relationships not only allow for spiritual growth and repair but also for a simplification of the complex sexual constructs in our minds. Celibacy takes the focus off of sex as the main form of intimacy in relationships, but if you're headed toward marriage, sex will obviously be a very new territory for the two of you. It is unrealistic to believe that you will jump into bed with your new spouse fully aware of how to please them sexually; irrespective to the number of partners you may have had in the past. Sex isn't, or at least it shouldn't be, a one-size-fits-all experience. Understanding the spiritual side of intimacy means we gain a greater appreciation and respect for the sacredness of sex. So it's just as important to discuss sex and pleasure openly with your mate as it is to maintain your covenant of celibacy in the relationship.

The two ideas are not dichotomous and can truly occur in the same context. You simply must enter the conversation with maturity, knowing that the purpose is not for your arousal, or to initiate flirtation that leads to sex. Think of this conversation as simply learning another dimension of your partner. This conversation should be done in relationships that you are sure are leading to marriage—as in you've discussed marriage in terms specific to a marriage between the two of you on a more than vague basis. This includes discussion on what your marriage will look like in respect to potential children, and/or the blending of families, residence, religious and social beliefs, and the like. Sexual pleasure should not be the initiating discussion of marital behavior between you and your partner.

The conversation of sexual pleasure is on-going and shouldn't feel forced of uncomfortable. If you're not comfortable *discussing* sex with your partner you are likely uncomfortable *having* sex with them as well. Being uncomfortable doesn't necessarily mean something is wrong, it simply means your relationship may need a bit more growth. It could also indicate that you may need to revisit your concepts about sex. If you are, like me, a woman of color, studies have shown grim outlooks of our intricacies regarding sexual attitudes. Studies have shown that we as Black women are far more restrictive of our sexuality, tend to enjoy sex less, and fail to explore other avenues of sexuality.[4] Further, Black women often view sex as the sole weapon in finding the balance of power with men. We have been conditioned to forsake physical pleasure in sex in favor of gaining emotional permanence and power[5] in a world that leaves us otherwise powerless due to our gender. In order to have a healthy relationship with our sexuality, we have to set aside these dysfunctions! In removing sex, celibate relationships strip the one way in which men and women try to control the other, and force a real development of trust and balanced power in the relationship, which helps to bring some function to our dysfunctional sexual attitudes.

A conversation about pleasure with our partner requires an open mind. Ask what they like, what have they enjoyed sexually up to this

---

[4] Burgest, D.R. (1990). Sexual games in Black male/female relations. *Journal of Black Studies, 21*(1), 103-116.

[5] Gonzales, A.M., & Rolison, G. (2005). Social oppression and attitudes toward sexual practices. Journal of Black Studies, 35(6), 715-729.

point in their life that they've either discovered through self-love or sex, and what a sex life would look like with you after you're married. I know it seems like this isn't a conversation that a celibate couple should have, but as I mentioned previously, you cannot take for granted that what you find to be satisfying pleases your mate as well! Sex comes in many flavors from the safety of vanilla, to the bold taste of a scoop of habanero banana, and everything in between, with some flavors blending better together than others.

In my relationship, my SO and I have had many conversations about what sex would look like after marriage. We've shared the things that we find to be pleasurable, our mutual fears of experiencing sex with one another for the first time, and what will likely be off limits sexually. It is important to note that our boundaries have been drawn simply by what we find to be erotically pleasing, not by what has been deemed as "safe sexual desire." The marriage bed is undefiled (Hebrews 13:4) so with the exception of adding in other people, throw out your notions of what makes safe Christian sex. Never fear or dismiss consenting sexual acts because social norms have deemed it as an indicator of latent homosexuality or some deep perversion. The key is consenting acts between two adults, so I'm not giving a pass to classified perversions by the DSM-IV (manual to diagnose mental disorders used by those in psychology), by the way! The only thing that makes a sexual act or desire gay is having sex with someone of the same gender—

that's it! Be open to the idea that your partner is pleased by sexual acts that you have not yet experienced and it may end up becoming a pleasure of yours if you keep an open and curious mind.

Developing healthy sexual attitudes is beneficial at every stage in our life and is quite crucial to the healthy growth of our romantic relationships. A healthy sex life with your spouse is built on the foundation of understanding that God wants a pleasurable sex life for your marriage, and by understanding what your sexual pleasure is through self-love, and candid conversation with your partner. Just bear in mind that your conversations about sexual intimacy are nearly as sacred as the act itself. It is not meant to be shared with every person you think or hope is *the one*. Take some time to dismantle the complications you have built up over time regarding your sexual nature; you're going to need it as you enter engagement and head towards marriage and the end of your celibacy! Even if you are not celibate for and until marriage, devoting time to the development and maturity of your sexual attitudes is invaluable as you walk your journey.

9: FAST YOUNG GIRLS, HOES, AND JEZEBELS

Unraveling our complexities about sex includes deconstructing the ways in which we identify, label, and oppress women's sexuality. As soon as we hear of a woman whose sexual life outpaces our own or falls outside of our comfort zone, we label her a hoe. We call our young women "fast" when they begin to express their sensual nature simply through their state of being a body that experiences puberty. Yes, we love to call a young woman whose budding body is feeling its first pangs of real human sexuality *fast* or *hot in the a*** for feelings she has little control over. Jezebel, the historical stereotype of Black women as animalistic, promiscuous sexual deviants, has enabled us to maintain these pretenses about sexually active women. We have failed to give attention to the context and reasoning that accompanies our sexual choices. Women who choose to sexually express themselves are quickly written off as whores who are unworthy of the privileges of being a "good woman." These sexual attitudes are unhealthy for the people who hold them and for the women and girls who are targeted by them.

The quickness that we have in labeling a woman as a whore or a young woman as fast is not a reflection of their sexual choices. It is a spotlight of our inability to have real conversations about sex, how we view and interpret sex, and that view's impact on our sexual decision-making. A study showed that "women were shown to favor casual relationships when the role of sex was to obtain independence and recreation through sex, to compensate for low feelings of self-worth (obtain affirmation), to meet expected societal images that encouraged women to be sexually available, as a method to segue into a monogamous relationship, as a way to move on from a previous sexual relationship, and to temporarily fill an emotional void."[6] Just think about that list of reasons for why women tend to have casual sex. Yes, women have sex because it feels good, but so does everyone, regardless of gender. When we move past that, however, it's evident that sex holds much deeper, complicated rationale for women. Still we've chosen to blanket these very real issues with the labels of "hoe", "fast", and "loose". Let's pull the covers back and get real about why we're having sex.

Pacifying Our Feelings

Sex is a way in which many people pacify feelings of inadequacy. This is especially true for women and young girls. So often, we use sex to

---

[6] Ann Kiki Anaebere, Adeline Nyamathi, Sally Maliski, Chandra Fo Angela Hudson, and Deborah Koniak-Griffin **She Decides: Sex Partner Selection Decision Making and African American Women** Journal of Black Studies November 2012 43: 872-892, fir published on September 12, 2012 doi:10.1177/0021934712459958

have our worth validated and affirmed. Regardless to how quickly the validation dissipates, it creates a dependency. How often have you had sex to bolster your confidence and attractiveness to a partner because you had feelings of low self-worth? Better question: can you trace those feelings of low self-worth to defining your worth by your sexual expression and ability to attract a mate? We have an overwhelming amount of cultural and social factors that influence our sexual decisions. One of which is our cultural tendency to shun singleness as a negative state. We have essentially made being a single woman of a certain age in our society a crime. We have made it more favorable to have a *piece* of a man or partner than to have none at all. This ostracizing of singleness can lead us to feel inadequate and develop low self-worth. A woman may have sex with multiple people to chase that fleeting feeling of affirmation and be labeled a hoe. We place the shame on her actions and not on the cultural and social factors that enable or encourage those actions—an action that is absolutely wrong and harmful. If you're struggling with feelings of self-worth, sex is not the answer. As I've stated before, sex is for your sacred pleasure and when you share that with the wrong person you may find yourself worse off than when you started. Celibacy is an excellent way to take inventory of your emotional inadequacies and deal with them without interference.

Lady in the Streets, Freak in the Sheets

Women enter an "it's complicated" relationship with sex practically from the time we are born. Women are primed from birth to deny sensual pleasure. We are encouraged to wait and hold on to our virginities for dear life in order to be considered a "good girl" who becomes a "good woman" eligible for marriage. At the same time men are encouraged to pursue women ruthlessly, a cultural facet that has given birth to rape culture (the desensitization of rape via perpetrator sympathizing, victim blaming, and rationalization of the violent act) and street harassment (being hit on by men despite declining offers, cat calls, and other sexually-motivated harassment in public spaces).

If you don't think that these primers for men and women begin in childhood, consider this: think about the birth of a baby boy and a baby girl. What are the things that you hear said about each one before their cognitive skills have even fully developed? "He's going to be a little heartbreaker! He's going to get all the girls," they exclaim over the boy child. Still, you're likely to hear "You're going to need a shotgun to keep them off of her" as they dote over the girl child. It doesn't end there, however. Young boys are praised for their mannish behaviors and their ability to attract women is prized and lovingly adored. Young girls, however, are already trained to act "lady like", pious, and subservient. Young girls are not encouraged to be loud, boisterous, or womanish as often. Then puberty comes along and the primers become even more conflicting. Parents who are glad that they cannot be impregnated and "bring home a baby" prize budding young men. Young men get conversations about condom usage and safe sex; young women get threats about getting pregnant and being fast. Teenage girls are often considered too young to have a boyfriend or express any kind of sexual intimacy but teenage boys are encouraged to mount anything with a pulse. The most interesting thing about this culture is that no one stops to question basic logic: if boys are encouraged and support in expressing sexuality and girls are not, *who* are they supposed to have sex with assuming they're straight?

So we find ourselves as grown women grappling with what we've been taught by our culture and also what our culture expects from us: to be women who are expertly sexual and available. We are expected to behave in a socially acceptable lady-like fashion while knowing how to be voracious vixens that provide endless pleasure to our partners. We walk a fine line of being a good woman with good sex, and a freak hoe with superb sex—and we do so without question. We not only accept being labeled as whores, but we label other women, encouraging this belief that these social expectations of our sexuality are acceptable!

We cannot have healthy sexual attitudes when we think of sex as the prize. We cannot hold on to the belief that we are better than another woman by stigmatizing her sexual behavior. Whether you have one sexual partner or a thousand—an ungodly soul tie created by sex holds the same level of consequence. Celibacy is not designed to help you "keep your body count low" and place you a notch above the rest. If you're still walking around emotionally broken due to unhealed hurts and distorted sexual attitudes, you still don't make a worthy partner. We must remove the idea of sexual purity or chastity as a method of pleasing and securing a man and understand our sacred sex as being a gift to provide us both balance and pleasure with the right partner.

I Need Love

We're having sex not because we're whores, but because we've been so ingrained with the idea that being single is a crime so we use our sex to communicate a desire for a relationship. We will have sex even when what we're using sex to communicate isn't heard. A recent study concluded that the included sample of African American women "pursued casual sexual relationships even [though the] women reported that they desired a committed relationship with the male, but the male preferred a relationship of a casual nature." The same study found that "some women pursued a casual sexual relationship in the hope that they will eventually transition into a monogamous relationship. Casual sexual relationships were seen as an intermediate step to monogamy and...attempt (with the passage of time) to convince their male partner to enter a monogamous relationship."[7]

We've been groomed to find and maintain a partnership as soon as we reach the age of consent practically. Because of this, we are having sex without titles but being labeled as a whore when we go from sexual relationship to relationship, using our limited knowledge of sexual intimacy to communicate desires and intent to our partners. Women who are highly sexually active are not whores; they are working within a broken system of heteronormative patriarchy (straight male system of oppression through power and domination). In heterosexual relationships, men's preference for monogamy is consistently the influencing factor male-female relationships. If a man says he just wants sex, often we as women will give in even when we want more. We will lie beneath you hoping that it means more than sex, and pick up the pieces when your words and actions tell us that it simply is not. We have sex because we've been left empty and broken by a previous relationship to which we gave our all. We have sex to escape loneliness, sadness, disappointment, and every other feeling in between. Yet, we choose only to add confusion to the sexual attitudes of women with our societal labels while excusing and even heralding the men who enable these behaviors.

We as women will never have positive relationships with sex until we begin to think

---

[7] (See #6)

critically about the role sex plays in our lives and of the expectations placed on us by society. We must take charge of our sexuality as a form of self-agency and liberation. Though I strongly advocate celibacy, it is still necessary to take charge by defining your sexual decisions for your pleasure and happiness. Who you are in totality is greater than what you have to offer sexually. Women do not have to settle for casual sex when we really want monogamous relationships. We do not have to settle for halfhearted emotional commitment when we want the whole heart. We don't have to settle for being labeled a whore or feeling unworthy because we don't live up to certain social expectations. We do this by holding our sisters and ourselves accountable in how we label and oppress each other while demanding that men take responsibility for their role in perpetuating these oppressions through the system of patriarchy.

10: THE ESCAPE HATCH

There comes a point in every conversation where you have to put down the points of morality and meet people in the condition and state that they are in. So far in this dialogue, I've shared with you the many oscillating points of sex and celibacy in our singleness and relationships. You may even be at a point where, if not already celibate, you are giving celibacy a serious consideration or your choice in celibacy has been strengthened. However, I cannot go a step further in our talk without being real in the fact that celibacy, the choice to become and to remain, is difficult. It is not my intention to paint celibacy as a decision whose path resembles "we fell in love, remained celibate, got married, and then lived happily ever after" because if you internalize this decision as such, you will be sorely disappointed with the process.

Celibacy is a catharsis of self-awareness and will show you, with exceeding clarity, how your behaviors and attitudes direct the outcomes of your intimate relationships. With your legs closed and spirit open to the direction of God, you are fed manna that will begin to deal with many of the issues and baggage that you've accumulated to this point in your life. While celibacy is not a solid path or guarantee of marriage, I hope I have illuminated so far how celibacy interplays from your singlehood into your relationships and eventually into your marriage and engagement.

There is no escape hatch in choosing to commit to celibacy. It is not a decision that you can commit to casually and hope to escape the wounds that premature sex brings. Of course, there are those of us who choose to be celibate only for a specific time period (e.g. until a specific anniversary date, a birthday, holiday, etc.) or those who believe celibacy is only best during certain phases of a relationship. While your act of obedience through celibacy at any level and for any length of time is honored, do not deceive yourself into the belief that your casual commitment to this covenant will protect you from the ramifications of your decision to have sex prematurely. I don't mean your usual "you're going to hell" condemnation when we have premarital sex. As my significant other often says, "We are not punished *for* our sins but *by* our sins." Keep in mind all of the signs of ungodly soul ties to get a sense of the consequences you can anticipate. You will experience the emotional turmoil that is bore of the energy created by sex, it is inescapable even if you do it at the mature point of your relationship (marriage). The difference, however, is that having sex in the maturity of God's timing equips you with the spiritual strength to deal with these new feelings appropriately.

The goal of this conversation is not to condemn those who do not live out their celibacy as I do. As I said in the preface, you may not ever make the decision to become celibate until marriage. You always have a free will decision to have sex—God gives you free will and I am not one to impede or infringe upon that. You probably have more examples in your life of sexually intimate relationships that became marriages, than celibate relationships that have become marriages, given the pervasive nature of premarital sex in our society. People marry every day from sexually intimate relationships and go on to have long, lasting marriages. Yet if you ever get into detailed conversations where they are open and honest, you will find out how much tension and strain caused in their pre-marital relationship was carried over into that marriage and it took a lot of faith and prayer to work through it. Entering a marriage after celibacy doesn't preclude you from all issues; it simply precludes you from *most* issues that come as a direct result of emotions born of sexual energy exchange.

After losing my virginity in my first relationship at the age of twenty, I thought I could casually commit to celibacy. I believed that if I knew the person at least a year prior to having sex with them, the relationship would be mature enough to withstand the emotional depth that would surely come after sex. It took two more sexual partners and a celibate relationship to figure out how wrong I was. In my first sexual relationship, I felt that since he was my first, my sex conveyed my expectations of his loyalty and respect to me. I never actually opened my mouth and conveyed my expectations, I assumed sex showed him that I trusted, respected, and loved him and deserved the same in return. So when he would do something to betray that expectation, the first thing out of my mouth during an argument was "you wasn't saying that when you was up in me!" How many times have you said that in the heat of anger with a sexual partner? Too often, we as women expect to have power over our partner's loyalty to our expectations through our sex. How many times have you heard or said yourself "oh, ain't nothing wrong with her 'cept she need some dick"? Men tend to expect that their sex controls the emotional behavior and reactions of women. With both partners trying to vie for power, the relationship becomes a power struggle laden with tension from not only normal growing pains of love but also the struggles that come from the exchange of sexual energy.

Never once in my sexual relationships, where I applied my casual celibacy commitment, did I ever successfully convey my expectations through sex. It was not until I committed wholly to celibacy that I began to transparently see who and what I was as a woman in relationships. I had a host of unresolved issues that I carried from one relationship to the other. Until I stopped relying on sex for intimacy, I was unable to be emotionally vulnerable in my relationships, which kept me from happiness in romance. Removing sex meant I had to stop blaming every failure in my relationships on the other person; I had to acknowledge and become accountable to those failures that fell on me. *This* is what celibacy will do for you—provide a looking glass of your innermost self while forcing you to address and fix those things that are broken.

Old habits die hard, though. The struggle for power in relationships doesn't just up and disappear because sex is absence. My SO and I still had struggles of power in our relationship. I do believe, however, that our commitment to celibacy allowed us grow into a place where being a *partner* took precedence over the need for power. I learned how to communicate my expectations and the absence of sex meant that I couldn't make excuses when he failed to meet them simply because the sex was so good. Celibacy doesn't mean that we don't argue, experience hurt at the hands of the other, or get pushed to our breaking point! It does mean, however, when we return to the table to reconcile that it comes from a place of genuine contrition. In my previous sexual relationships, apologies would be offered up simply because one or both of us wanted to get back to our sex life, not necessarily because the issue had been truly processed and resolved. So no, my celibacy commitment has not been a walk in the park but it has done what it should do: be a catharsis of self-awareness.

Just as there is no escape hatch out of a real and complete commitment to celibacy, celibacy itself is not an escape hatch from the risk of love and relationships. Sometimes we use our celibacy as a defense against dealing with emotional baggage and risking hurt in a new relationship.

We can be fresh into the dating scene again and on every first few dates, we make it a point to declare our celibacy to make it clear that if a person is only looking for sex they should look elsewhere. In itself, this isn't problematic but you have to ask yourself what your motivation behind it is. Some may simply prefer to only date others who are celibate, as another celibate person tends to better understand the process than someone who is not. This is a phenomenal situation to find yourself in and means that you won't have to do as much groundwork in establishing your celibate relationship. As long as you remember that understanding the process as partners doesn't make either of you impervious to sexual temptation and continue to strive towards holding one another for your covenant, you're in great shape.

Yet when you declare your celibacy early on simply because you don't want to deal with the drama of a relationship because of lingering hurts from a past relationship, you need to check your defense. Not only do you possibly kill a potentially great romantic relationship with an early declaration, you assume off the bat that the person you're dating has no interest in you beyond sex. That doesn't give much credit to them or to you! Do you honestly believe that you are not interesting enough outside of sex to attract and keep a potential mate? If not, then you may need to revisit the looking glass and figure out what motivates these negative thoughts you have of yourself. As I mentioned before, not every early declaration of celibacy is a sign of emotional baggage—but you'd better be positively sure it is not! If your potential mate isn't celibate, what more of a wonderful opportunity could you ask for to minister to someone about the life-changing deliverance that is celibacy? Even if you don't end up together, the seed you plant in their spirit will forever remain. *That* is far more important to the building of the kingdom—sharing with someone the transformative power of Christ in our lives!

Ultimately, *Closed Legs Do Get Fed* isn't here to give you a loophole in your celibacy commitment. At the same time, it is also not here to condemn you to hell if you should choose not to commit to celibacy. You've gotta work out your own soul salvation just like I work out mine (Philippians 2:12 NLT). It is merely here to discuss the struggle of this life choice in a way that is refreshingly candid and real. Sex is a phenomenal act of intimate exchange, it feels great when done right, but it does have its consequences. Celibacy is a struggle, it's not easy, but it does have its rewards. Whatever decision you ultimately make for your life, just know that while there is no escape hatch from the consequences of our choices, "God is working in you, giving you the desire and the power to do what pleases Him" (Philippians 2:13 NLT).

Reflection Questions for Chapters 8-10

The following questions are presented for the sake of introspection and to guide discourse among couples and friends. You are welcome to continue reading the book without answering— no one is keeping score!

1. What, if any, are some of the hang-ups you have about sex due to religious teachings? Do you feel you need to overcome any of them to have healthier sexual attitudes?

2. How comfortable are you with having sexually intimate discussions with a partner, a family member, or friends? If you have any level of discomfort with any of these people, why?

3. If you are currently wavering on a celibacy decision, what factors keep you from committing fully to celibacy?

4. If you are celibate, what has celibacy revealed to you about yourself and your actions in romantic relationships?

5. Have you ever had a casual celibacy commitment as described in Chapter 9? In what ways have you benefitted or suffered from that decision?

6. How often do you use sex as a means of control and power? How often has it worked to your full advantage— meaning you got everything you wanted from it?

11: I'M CELIBATE, NOW WHAT?

So you've made the decision to be single and celibate, congratulations! What now? This is a question we often ask ourselves after removing sex from our lives. We can tend to focus so much on the spiritual that we forget we're still natural beings that have to actively participate in the world around us! I've spent quite a bit of time discussing how removing sex will alter your spiritual and emotional self, but in order to be fully equipped you must know what to do with yourself after the bible (or bible app if you're a techie like myself!) is closed.

One of the greatest things you can do while single is getting your financial health in order. Though it sounds boring, robust financial health is important regardless of relationship status! If you're hoping to find a relationship in the future, it is worth noting that financial management is a huge source of ire for many couples. Being single is a wonderful time to improve your credit score. Credit scores range from 300 to 850 and a fair, average credit score is between 630 and 699[8]. This score may vary vastly with each of the three credit bureaus and should be monitored frequently. A single point can mean the difference between prime (low interest) and subprime (high interest) loan rates. No one is entirely sure how the scoring system works aside from Fair Isaac

---

[8] Credit Karma http://www.creditkarma.com

Corporation (FICO) but late payments, high balances, hard inquiries (applying for credit such as credit cards, cars, and mortgages) and charged off accounts (accounts closed due to non-payment after six months of first date of non-payment) tend to lower your score while low balances, high card limits, and on time payments will raise your credit score. Credit repair, depending on the amount of damage you've done so far, is a lengthy and arduous process. So it's an excellent one to undertake while you're single since you only have to be concerned with your household's financial needs. If you haven't already, get copies of all three of your credit reports and scores so you have a foundation to work from for any necessary repair. While single, it is a good idea to start a personal savings and/or IRA [individual retirement account], take advantage of your employer's full-match 401k incentives, learning how to best budget and manage your household bills, and to start spending less than what you earn. Now I know what you're saying, this all sounds phenomenal in theory. I know many of us are or have been members of the working poor class during our lives. For example, a car is not a luxury but a necessity for many of us. If you haven't had the money to save to buy a car outright, you will need to finance. If you have poor credit, you will be penalized with high interest rates and payments. The cycle of the punishment of poverty doesn't end with just car interest but continues with auto insurance (credit score contributes to rate determination), credit cards, home and personal loans, and even rent! Is it all one monumental numbers game? Absolutely, but it is yet still one we must successfully learn to play to get the financial footing we need for the things we desire in life.

Physical health is another aspect that can be improved upon while you're single. It is important to note that I don't encourage the improvement of physical appearance for the purposes of being phallic-centric or more simply, for the purpose of being attractive to a man. For one, this would imply that women should have no vested interest in their personal appearance simply for wanting to find themselves attractive. Secondly, taking care of our physical health should be seen as a form of self-love! Improving your physical health is not inextricable from weight loss. You can become more physically active without the intent to lose weight—and that's perfectly fine! The numbers on your blood pressure readings, cholesterol scans, and other biometric checks matter more than what is on the scale. The focus on self-improvement through achieving good health should come before losing weight. Obviously, if you're a person who is self-conscious about your size or has issues regarding self-image physical activity and weight loss may provide a much needed confidence boost. Doing it while single means you don't have to account to a mate or spouse about your dietary changes and new workout habits—not to mention you don't have to worry about if a mate/spouse is satisfied with your health progress! Physical health improvement while single is a time to be selfishly consumed with self-interest for your health without apology.

While you're single and celibate, carpe diem! Being single allows you to live in the moment without obligation! Not only does it lessen your chances of feeling that you sacrificed some portion of your life when you enter a relationship, it will provide wonderful stories of your lived experience to recount to others! Spend some time planning and taking trips. The trips don't have to be to extravagant lands and destinations; often there are things in our own neighborhood that we haven't bothered to check out because we're so busy! Check out your local historical landmarks or explore the Victoria Falls of Zambia. Only your finances and imagination limit your travels! Being single means you can tick off things on your bucket list that would be hindered by a relationship, take advantage of last minute plans with friends, and take the opportunity to get to know others while making friends outside of your comfort zone. While you shouldn't do anything that would put your life or celibacy at risk, go the whole yard and experience life!

Develop your own interests and hobbies while you're single! Most of us live within our limited world experience. Being single is a time to get out and explore the world! It could be something as simple as committing to try new dishes at your favorite restaurants each week or picking up a new book by a different author or genre. If you've wanted to learn a new language, pick up that language-learning app on your phone or tablet or check into a class offered at your community centers. Not only will developing your own interests expand your cultural awareness, it expands your self-awareness. When you're confident in you, it spills over into every single aspect of your life!

While you're single, be sure to spend plenty of time with your family and friends! Join a singles' group either at church or just by linking up with fellow singles in your circle of friends. Don't forget to hang out with your coupled friends and family too! Whoever you choose to spend time with, spend quality time cultivating those friend/kinships. These people can (and likely will) be your community of support through your celibacy commitment and future relationships!

Being single is also a wonderful time to develop a spirit of philanthropic service to others. 1 Corinthians 7:8 says that it is better for those of us who are unmarried to remain as such so that we may give our undivided service to Christ and the Kingdom of Heaven. Of course that chapter goes on to talk about how it is better to marry than to burn with desires of the flesh so I'm not saying you need to be single forever. However, while we are single, we should recognize that it allows us to be of service in a way that those who are coupled cannot be. While you are single, your volunteerism is unimpeded by the demands of household and spouses! So if you're looking for things to do that might help others, look for volunteer opportunities with organizations whose mission and goals compliment your skill set and beliefs. It is a greater blessing to give than it is to receive (Acts 20:35 NLT) and community service through volunteerism is one of the simplest ways we are able to give to others.

Finally, being single is a great time to create self-focused goals. During this time, you can bring a sense of direction to your life. These goals could be as long or short as you would like. If you have a dream job, maybe it's time to map out an attainable path towards making dream into reality. Have a habit such as smoking or a coffee addiction and want to shake it? Take some time to map out steps towards beating these habits! Being single means your only concern is you (and your children if you have them, of course!) so take full advantage of it!

Of course, these things just scratch the surface of things that you can take advantage of while being single and celibate. The takeaway, however, is that there is more to your accomplished adult life than your sexual skill and prowess. Removing sex from your life while single will not mean that you'll lead a life of boredom while waiting [im]patiently for your spouse so you can get your celibacy commitment over with! As I stated in earlier chapters, take full advantage of your time being single to focus on yourself because selfishness must be checked at the door when you enter your next romantic relationship!

12: WE'RE CELIBATE, NOW WHAT?

It's only fair that couples who are reading this book are also equipped with "what to do in the absence of sex" knowledge as well. Keeping sex out of relationships while maintaining the vigor and vitality is just as hard, if not harder, as when we're single. Don't fret, I promise there are still many things you and your boo can do while celibate and in relationship that will keep the fire of intimacy roaring in your relationship.

The most underrated form of intimacy in relationships is communication. In the absence of sex, great dialogue between partners will build a love that rivals even the most torrid of sexual romances. Open communication allows us to get to know our partner's heart, which will in turn draw your hearts closer to one another. There are a series of conversation topics that I believe every couple should have to truly discover who they're dating. These topics include discussion about your pasts, your trust for one another, and communication. As your relationship matures, many of these conversations will flow naturally but it never hurts to prompt these discussions when you feel led!

It is said that the past predicts the future. However, I believe that our past is an indicator of things that we may need to fix in order to *improve* our future. When maturing in your relationship, it is important to understand your partner's childhood and romantic past. Ask questions to understand how their childhood experiences have shaped their behavior and attitude. You should definitely ask about their relationship with their parents and siblings, if they have any. A person who has unresolved conflict with a parent may be easily triggered by struggles and conflict in relationships. Essentially, if your partner has a bad relationship with their mom, your behaviors as a woman may trigger negative response and vice versa for fathers and men. It is not something that can't be overcome, but it is something that must be addressed head-on. Ask if your partner has ever experienced physical, sexual, or emotional abuse during their childhood. Someone who has experienced abuses of this nature must be dealt with using a *lot* of patience and prayer if they haven't been delivered from the traumas attached to this type of abuse. If you feel you are incapable of handling this responsibility, knowing this information will give you a good assessment of if the relationship is a good fit for you. Childhood inquiries don't have to be solely limited to asking about negative experiences – be sure to ask them about their most fond memories of their childhood and how it is has shaped their outlook on life. Also, it is necessary to ask if your partner has a judicial or criminal past and asking them about it in detail if they do. For some, criminality is a deal breaker for whatever reason.

When asking about a romantic past, it's good to find out what signaled the ending of their past romantic relationships. Ask what they liked and disliked most about their exes, what they think an ex would say about them if asked, and if they've ever been physically or emotionally violent in past relationships. This not only helps you see if you possess qualities that have typically ended your partner's past relationships, it will also give you an indication of what you can and cannot handle. Domestic Violence is never okay—at the hands of men **or** women—but not everyone who has ever been violent will be violent in every relationship. However, if your partner has a violent past, be sure to probe deep enough to figure out if it is *truly* their past or if that's simply their character. When discussing your pasts, it is important to understand that you or your partner may choose to withhold certain things. You must decide for yourself if you can continue your relationship knowing that you or your partner is unwilling to share part of their past with you.

Trust is also a necessary area of communication. Trust is something that is built by conversation, and iterated by action, so in order to know actions to commit we must know what factors our partner is looking for in the area of trust. The number one area is usually the ability to be monogamous. Ask your partner if they've ever cheated on or been cheated on by a previous partner as it will tell you quite a bit about their attitudes toward cheating. If they were the cheater, ask them what prompted them to cheat. One thing we fail to remember is that while cheating is ultimately the *choice* of the cheater,

99

both partners contribute to the volatile atmosphere that makes one partner feel that cheating is an option. Learning what failures occurred in previous relationships will serve you well in avoiding them in your current relationship. If they have been cheated on, ask them how the experience made them feel and affected their attitudes towards relationships. Finally, ask your partner if they've ever felt insecure due to your behaviors with others outside of your relationship. Sometimes, we do things that trigger feelings and insecurities within our partners without even knowing it. When discussing trust in general, ask if your partner automatically starts with a full trust cup that empties with every incident that breaks trust or if their trust cup starts empty and is filled by the actions of a partner who has earned it. Trust is the foundation of any relationship. Much like a home sinks with a cracked foundation, a relationship will quickly capsize with broken trust.

Communication is a topic that requires—you guessed it—communication! You will need to decide how you will deal with conflict. Ask your partner about their argument style, learning if they like to discuss problems immediately at the point of conflict or wait until they are more levelheaded to talk it out. Ask your partner how you can best communicate your feelings without bringing them offense, or harm, and if they feel that there is any reason that they cannot, or don't want to talk to you. Ask your partner how they feel about communicating with others about the conflicts of your relationship and, if it's okay, to whom are those conversations limited. You should be sure that you're able to talk to your partner about any and everything but also be aware of any limitations if they exist. A relationship with poor communication is a relationship doomed to fail!

So when you're not doing all that chattering, what do you do together? With modification, you can do many of the same things you did as a single person with your partner! If you spent your single time getting into physical shape, you can now share those activities with your partner. You don't have to share your #GymFlow time with them, but you can try new physical adventures like rock climbing, hiking, biking, running 3 and 5ks, and all sorts of physical endurance activities if your partner is into those things as well! If they aren't into it but interested, it may be an opportunity to introduce them to a hobby of yours and adopt them to it at a pace that's comfortable for them. If they aren't at all interested, it's just as well! It is important for us to maintain our personal identities in relationships so keeping some separate activities and hobbies will help us to not lose the "me" in "we" within our relationships.

You can still plan and take trips with your partner; vacations aren't just for single people and families! There are many vacations you can plan and take with your mate that are romantic without sex. Maybe you both have a shared destination you'd like to visit, by all means you should! Being celibate doesn't preclude being able to travel and spend time together. While it may require modified adjustments depending on how your celibacy looks, couples' vacations add to the richness of your relationships while growing your love and creating memories.

Being in a relationship that is celibate also allows us to cultivate shared hobbies and interests. While there are some things that are better done single, there are still wonderful things that are better done together. Maybe you both love films, why not become movie aficionados and watch a wide gamut of films together at home, retail theaters, and small film houses? Maybe you're both foodies, love gaming, love books, or love watching the Sunday football game. Whatever your shared interests are, doing it together is a rich experience that indulges your *both* your interests and allows you to spend quality time together and fall more in love *without* sex.

Spending time with your friends and family while in a relationship is just as critical as doing so while single. When we're in relationships, we can get so caught up in being with our significant others that we spend less time cultivating the friend/kinships with others in our lives. This can lead to our family and friends holding resentment from our lack of attention and lessening of their much-needed support in our lives. Failing to balance the scales can lead to feelings of isolation and strain within the relationship. Your significant other isn't meant to fill the void of every single role in your life! In order to find balance between time with your boo and time with your folks, try setting aside a few days a month or one day a week that is solely focused on spending time with your family and friends doing activities you tend to enjoy with them. Cultivating these key roles in your life is important not only to your personal sanity but the health and longevity of your relationship!

Still there is the option of, depending on your intimacy boundaries, good old fashion date nights out or in the house. There's nothing sweeter than spending a night out on the town with the one you love. If you're like my SO and me, you actually end up watching crazy YouTube videos and binge watching shows on Netflix. The goal isn't the activity, however, it's the time spent simply being in the presence of someone you love. The moment we begin to find it a struggle to even be around our significant others for a long period of time signals some issues in our relationships that must be resolved!

Much like being single and celibate, being in a celibate relationship is far from boarding the blah train to Boredomville. You simply learn that intimacy takes on a different, much deeper form that may force a level of transparency you've never experienced in a relationship before. Celibate relationships will not only strengthen you personally but they will give you the opportunity to discern a person's intent and your compatibility with them without giving of yourself more than you can stand to lose. It will take work but with faith and determination, you can keep the intimacy in your celibate relationship invigorated!

13: IN THE MEANTIME: WHAT TO EXPECT WHEN ENGAGED

Whether your proposal story is as simple as popping the question over dinner or as elaborate as a proposal atop the Eiffel Tower that became a viral Internet sensation, the outcome is the same. Someone proposed and one of you said yes, so congratulations on your impending nuptials. Right now is an amazingly exciting time in your life, between people clamoring to see your ring and being inundated with every wedding show, magazine, and expert advice, it is easy to lose sight of the real goal. Engagement is another depth of maturity in your relationship that leads you to your goal of becoming joined for life. However, there is still work to be done in order to be sure that you successfully make it to the altar. This chapter may propose some concepts that a few may be uncomfortable with but the hope is to open the dialogue about reconciling humanity with Christianity.

This period in your life is an easy time to forget that you're *engaged* and not married which may cause you to forget that you're still in this celibacy thing! Waiting for sex until marriage will likely increase your chances of a lasting marriage than those who choose to have sex before marriage. A recent study showed that if you've had more than one sexually intimate relationship in your life, there is an increased risk of divorce.[9] While the conclusions of that research may not phrase it quite the way I will, I believe this is solely due to our failure to sever the soul ties of our sexual past before entering marriage. You cannot carry the issues that the exchange of sexual energy causes into your marriage and expect uncomplicated success—even if you've managed to be celibate! Celibacy requires action beyond abstaining from sex; you have to deal with all the spirits that have attached themselves to you through sex. If you've gotten to the point of engagement, it is safe to say that your love has grown incredibly strong. With such a strong love, your inability to complete that love with the final step of intimacy may cause increased arguing at this stage of the relationship. As always, the resolution to this conflict is to remember the goals of your celibacy, pray for God's guidance, and rely on your faith and fortitude to see you through.

There is a controversial idea that I would like to put forth to couples that are engaged. You've worked very hard to establish and maintain your celibacy. Marriage as your next phase in life will come with its own trials, even after you are able to intimately connect. Chief among them is getting used to living with your spouse day in and day out. They say you never

---

[9] Teachman, J. (2003), Premarital Sex, Premarital Cohabitation, and the Risk of Subsequent Marital Dissolution Among Women. Journal of Marriage and Family, 65: 444–455. doi: 10.1111/j.1741-3737.2003.00444.x

fully know someone until you live with them—and it's true. You know this person's spirit, heart, and soul, at this point but you may not know that s/he likes to squeeze the toothpaste in the middle of the tube or leaves hair all over the sink when they shave. You may not know that they like the temperature in the house Antarctic cold, or Sahara hot, year round or that they like to refrigerate their syrup but leave out their ketchup. They may snore, sleep wildly, not be the best housekeepers, and other minor annoyances that you haven't had a clue of because you don't live together. These things, while minor by themselves, can be fodder for much larger arguments during the adjustment period of newlywed life. It is the little foxes that spoil the vine (Song of Solomon 2:15 KJV) and is why I propose living together during a portion of your engagement. Wait, wait, and wait! Before you stone me, hear me out. First of all, I recognize this is not something that everyone can or will do—and it doesn't make your choice wrong. This is a choice only for those couples that have the willpower and commitment to remain celibate until marriage! Studies have shown that living together with someone who is your intended spouse is not associated with an increased risk of divorce.[10] The positive benefits of it are that you

---

[10] Teachman, J. (2003), Premarital Sex, Premarital Cohabitation, and the Risk of Subsequent Marital Dissolution Among Women. Journal of Marriage and Family, 65: 444–455. doi: 10.1111/j.1741-3737.2003.00444.x

will get to enjoy your partner's companionship, combined financial income, and escape walking into unchartered territories after marriage. You will learn each other's daily habits, routines, and quirks and grow accustomed to them before you give *I dos* to something you *don't* know if you can put up with! If you do choose this route, you need to have set date for the wedding and deposits made with pertinent vendors for the wedding. I would also not recommend doing this for more than 90 days before the wedding; you don't need to get comfortable in cohabitating and forgetting that you need to marry! It is of course possible to marry and be happy without living together, but I do want to present it as an option that can be exercised while maintaining your celibacy. Know what you and your relationship can withstand before committing to this decision.

Whether you decide to cohabitate or not, there are still crucial conversations you need to have with your fiancé(e) before getting married. These conversations include discussing your future as newlyweds, children, finances, and your life priorities including work and health. These conversations may be uncomfortable but they cannot and should not be avoided.

Since you're engaged you have probably spent a lot of time talking about your future in *getting* married but you may not have discussed *being* married in as much detail. While you are engaged, it is a good time to talk about your differences as individuals, and discover those differences that conflict and compliment you all as a couple. In discussing conflict, you will need to discuss how you will maintain the skills you've gained in your celibate relationship for conflict resolution in your marriage. Since you will be having sex as a married couple, it will be easy to fall back into the pattern of relying on sex as passive emotional engagement in your marriage! You should discuss how you would strike a balance with your marriage and your friend/kinships. In marriage not only will you have to continue to nurture your friend/kinships as individuals, you will have to learn how to accept your new family as well as how to split your time between the two. With respect to the future in your marriage, it is good to consider where you would both like to live, if moving away from your families is acceptable, and (if you have aging parents) if having either set of parents living with you is okay. These are all quite real considerations for the future of many couples and are worthy of discussing before getting down the aisle. Though your opinions may change as the years pass, having a solid understanding of where each of you stands is a solid foundation for your marriage.

Discussing your future family is probably one of the absolutely most important discussions you can have. Some of you will walk into marriages that create a blended family. You should discuss how you will handle discipline of one another's children, what the children will call the non-parental spouse, if you want more children together, and how to make a union of not only yourselves but your children as well. If you're both childless, you should establish if you want children, as marriage doesn't necessarily obligate you to birth children from your union. If you do want children, you should decide how many you would like to have, when you would be open to trying to conceive, and what options are acceptable if you're unable to conceive. If you do become parents, you should agree on discipline methods, if one of you stays home who it will be, religious and moral teachings, and what things about education you both value the most for your future children.

Financial management is the conversation that makes or breaks many relationships but it should not be avoided. You need to know what your financial portfolio looks like, from your credit scores to your savings account balances. You should have an open and honest conversation about all of your current personal debts, your ability to manage money, and how you intend to handle debts and obligations in the household. You will be combining resources, so your intended spouse deserves to know how well you can or cannot manage your money. Don't feel ashamed if you don't manage money well, if one of you manages money better than the other then they should take the financial lead in the relationship. If you both have poor money management skills, seek out help from free financial advisors and seminars that are held in your city or neighborhood. Finances and the strain that mismanagement can cause will easily rip apart a marriage. You should spend some significant time discussing how you will handle financial stress and strain, because even with the best management of money, financial devastation can happen through a job loss or medical bankruptcy. You should discuss your household budget, who will be responsible for paying which bills, joint savings and checking, and if you will retain your individual accounts in addition to joint accounts. These questions may seem like they can be put off until you actually begin to merge your finances but in reality, they will allow you to enter your marriage with an unfettered view of your financial situation.

Life happens while we aren't paying attention. Soon, the other obligations of our lives can take precedence over our marriage. That's why it is important to understand how your fiancé(e) prioritizes their life. You should discuss the importance and amount of time spent on your personal health goals, working extra hours on the job, with friends and family without your spouse, your children, and your spiritual life. You should be sure that your spouse puts their relationship and time with God above their relationship with you, but more importantly, you should be *okay* with that reality. You should decide your friends' and families' level of impact and involvement in your marriage, so that you both respect the bounds of your trust at all times. This is also a wonderful time to discuss physical and psychological health, as well as your views on the role of counseling and therapy in your life, in the face of issues.

Your time of engagement will be both blissful and stressful, but never forget that you're entering into another phase of ministry. Yes, marriage is a ministry that should bring glory to God. Your union should stand as a testimony that when you stand on the promises of God in obedience, it will be blessed. Blessed doesn't mean easy, it just means that it is covered by the hand of God! The points of consideration and conversation put forth in this chapter is healthy for any and every couple considering marriage and should be incorporated during any period of engagement.

So far we've walked through the stages of romance from singlehood to engagement, which is where many advices on marriage and relationships end. We like to think that all relationships, even with conflict, end happily ever after. However, some conflict just can't be overcome. What do we do then?

14: WHAT BECOMES OF THE BROKENHEARTED?

Not all of the relationships that we begin and nurture will grow into what we hope for them to be. Even under the best circumstances, some relationships will end in a breakup. Maybe your breakup is mutual and amicable, enabling you to move forward without missing a beat. If your breakup was not of your own choosing, you may be left with feelings of pain, misery, and brokenness that feel nearly irreconcilable. Though most breakups are tough, this is especially true when you have had a celibate relationship. You may have expected that since you were doing it God's way it would be bound to work. Still, your breakup may leave you with more questions than answers and despair so deep that you question your commitment to God, your celibacy, and yourself. This chapter will address how to work through grieving the loss of a relationship while rebuilding your mind, heart, and spirit.

In the wake of your heartache, you will feel a range of emotions from sadness of the loss, to anger that despite giving the best of yourself in the absence of sex, you're still left alone. It's a time to easily misdirect your anger towards God as well. After all, you did it all according to His plan including remaining faithful to your celibacy covenant. We have all been at a place of anger with God, so you're not in unfamiliar territory. Often we have been told that it's not okay to be angry with God, much less to be bold enough to make our anger heard to Him. However, that's exactly what you need you do: express your anger to God. You have to lay your whole heart before God, not just the portions that make you look like a perfect model Christian. Your prayer can be as simple as "God, I'm angry and I have so much frustration and hatred built up inside of me. I cannot carry these burdens in my heart or mind so I'm giving them to you. You told me in your word that if I cried out, you would heal me so I'm taking you at your word." When you close that prayer with your Amen, however, you need to realize that God's grace is without fault and everything He does is right, even when we don't agree. Your admission of anger and submission to His authority will bring a comforting peace. Though it may take some time to see how He will get the glory out of even this, you will see it and you won't regret being honest with God about your feelings. There are a few things that should be done after a breakup that, with the partnership of the Holy Spirit for clarity, will help you not only to heal but see God's grace and glory even in this.

After dealing with your anger toward God, you have to deal with your feelings about the loss you've suffered. It helps to begin by being honest about why the break up occurred. So often after a break up we only see how the other person contributed to the relationship disruption so we shift blame and bury our head in the sand to ignore that we too contributed! Being in a celibate relationship doesn't make you immune to the growing pains of a maturing relationship. Maybe you ignored the red flags that the relationship was soon reaching its demise. Maybe you were not as compromising as you should have been or maybe you two had failure of communication on critical issues to the success of your relationship. While I don't advise that you internalize all the blame, it takes the actions of *two* people to end a relationship.

While you spend time replaying past scenes from the relationship, be sure that you spend more time identifying the positive lessons that you learned than time spent on looping the heartbreak. Yes, the relationship has ended but the invaluable experience it has gifted you with should not. If nothing else, the relationship has taught you to recognize when communication has begun to fail and how to better articulate what you want and need in your next relationship. Further, it could have illuminated some unresolved emotional baggage that must be unpacked before going on to the next relationship. Even if the relationship felt like an emotional rollercoaster that left you vomiting your innards while tears streamed down your face, if it matured you then it was worth the time spent to make you a better version of you.

In considering what role you played in the ending of your relationship, consider if your standards are too high or too lax. When we spend too much time residing at either end of the spectrum, we miss out on possibly phenomenal relationships. Before you mind even thinks it: your celibacy commitment is not on the list of standards that are too strict so don't get it twisted. If your partner can't value your emotional commitment without sex then they aren't worth your time. If your other standards are too high, you will likely continue to be unhappy in your romantic relationships. While we all want someone who will best compliment us as partners, unrealistically high expectations will always cause someone who's simply being their human self to disappoint you. The perfect soul mate doesn't exist in some idealized standard form. The perfect person for you as God has determined it, may come in an imperfect form as you've imagined it. If your standards are too low, you will be too easily impressed with the bare minimum while disappointed because a person doesn't suddenly meet your idealized version of a great relationship partner. Ultimately, you must make sure your standards align with His standards and plan for your life.

One of the hardest things to accept in the breakup of a celibate relationship is that simply because a person is celibate or agrees to wait with you doesn't mean they are sent by God to be the one. Some people are simply quite patient, well for a while at least. They may agree to enter into a celibate relationship with you while assuming and hoping in the back of their mind that you will cave at some point. When they see that you aren't, they may lose their patience and leave the relationship.

That's the thing about celibacy (well, any obedience to God really): it will separate the wheat from the tare. Celibate relationships allow us to see who is really in it for the long haul and who is not. Regardless of what stage your celibate relationship reaches, even if it is engagement, if a person's intentions are not pure they will be revealed before God allows you to walk blindly into a lifelong commitment and suffer greater hurt.

To understand the previous point, you have to understand God's plan in rejection. One of the most powerful prayers we ever have prayed or will pray is The Lord's Prayer. So often we pray and sing this prayer with no consideration to its power but merely from perfunctory memorization. The prayer opens with "Our Father, which art in heaven, Hallowed be thy name. **Thy kingdom come, Thy will be done in earth as it is in heaven.**" This line is perhaps the hardest line to utter during this prayer. When we pray this prayer, we're turning over our will to the authority of God and acknowledging that He knows the beginning and the end, and in that He knows what is best for us. It says even in hurt, rejection, disappointment, and anger, "YOUR will God, not mine." It says YOUR ways, not my own. Our intellect will often try to usurp our faith, but our faith is the only thing that can cause God to make clear the things our intellect cannot decipher. What I love about the Lord's prayer, though, is that it answers God's plan in rejection: "And lead us not into temptation, but deliver us from evil:

117

For thine is the kingdom, and the power, and the glory, **forever.** Amen" (Matthew 6:13 KJV). God's rejection in our relationships is to deliver us from something that would hinder us from drawing near unto Him. When you ask for His will to be done in your life as He's ordained it in heaven, you can guarantee it will be accompanied by a breaking process from any and everyone who would stand in the way of His perfecting will. I know it because I'm living it! God's purpose in the rejecting my other relationships was so that I would gain the knowledge I needed to write this book. I spent so much time wondering why I wasn't good enough for my previous romantic partners to change and grow with me. However in writing this very chapter, I've realized that I was not only good enough but that God had a purpose much higher than settling me into any of my previous relationships. He needed me to go through the pains of repeated rejection and then obedience and deliverance through celibacy so that I could "go out into the highways and hedges" (Luke 14:23 KJV) and compel someone just like me to come into the knowledge that God's plan for our lives is much greater than any plan we could set out and complete alone. If He thinks that highly of me, to use my pain for His glory, despite what I am and have been, know that He feels the same about you and has an equally amazing plan in your rejection.

After you come to accept your faults and understand God's plan, don't be so quick to jump in the next relationship. You should take as much time as you need to heal and re-evaluate. Use this time to remain committed to yourself through the obedience of your celibacy commitment or even to make a commitment of celibacy if you haven't already. You need this time to be sure that you do not allow this breakup define who you are. Simply because one relationship ended doesn't mean that you are not worthy of love. Jumping too fast into the next relationship could cause you to miss out on critical points of healing that would only cause suffering in your next relationship.

Finally, you should accept the breakup and find peace to move forward with your life. The hardest part of finding peace is to do so in the absence of answers. You have to accept that you may never get answers from your ex(es) over why your relationship ended. In order to move forward, however, you have to place forgiveness even where it is undeserved. If we fail to forgive others we not only cause God to not forgive us for our trespasses but we block ourselves from the peace of closure. Finding peace after a breakup may take some work but it will assure that you're not zipping up another suitcase of emotional baggage to weigh you down, as you continue your journey.

So what becomes of the brokenhearted? With God, they find peace and comfort in knowing that His will does not intend to leave you forever broken and hurting. Know that walking the right road that God has for your life means that you may lose a few along the way but what

God rewards you with for your obedience will replace those losses with much more.

15: FINDING HOPE

You've journeyed with me through this book in my testimonies of love, loss, finding myself, and loving again. At this point, maybe you've seen some of yourself in me and maybe you haven't. Regardless of where you stand and if you've made your celibacy decision or you haven't, hearing the testimonies of others reassures us that we are not alone in our feelings and experiences. In this chapter, I will present to you the testimonies of three women in my life. I am almost certain the majority of you will see yourself in at least one or all of them—I know that I do!

Claire, Zaria, and Kamille[11] are a well-rounded trio of educated, saved women whose journeys are as different as they are alike. Claire is a twenty-something single mother of two who holds three degrees and a corporate job with a Fortune 100 company. She is also *Miss Single & Considering* as she's currently single yet still sexually active without a history of consistent celibacy. After some self-reflection, she has arrived at a place in her life where she's seriously considering celibacy as a decision to change her

---

[11] Names have been changed to protect the personal identities of the individuals involved. The views and opinions of this book may not reflect the personal views of these individuals except where otherwise noted.

spiritual walk. Zaria is a thirty-something who holds two degrees and a blazing career that has yet to reach its zenith even after nearly a decade of work experience. She is also *Miss Single & Celibate* after the ending of her last romantic relationship and previous celibacy experience. Finally, Kamille is a young newlywed who recently finished undergrad and is exploring her other talents and gifts that would make room for her in a way that allows her to be both financially profitable and a vessel for God to use in ministry. She serves as *Mrs. Married from Celibacy* in this conversation as her recent nuptials came after a whirlwind engagement and celibate courtship. As you read their stories, it is our shared prayer that you not only see your past and present self in them but that you are also able to see your future self in them.

***

"I've always had questions regarding celibacy, but it seems to be taboo in the church where I'd think that I'd find help and answers. Most importantly, I haven't understood how to discuss celibacy with my mate without sounding crazy!" – Claire, Miss Single & Considering

Claire, who has been single for eight months, recently ended a tumultuous 15-month relationship that was according to her "full of infidelity." In a sordid twist, her last relationship was not ended simply by her discovery of infidelity but her ex simply vanished for two weeks before reappearing married to his mistress. Devastated and left with more questions than answers, Claire began to turn more to her relationship with God that she'd strayed so far from. Like so many of us, Claire had a belief in God and had even professed salvation but allowed life to come in and cause her to forget to nurture and nourish the relationship. As her spiritual walk strengthened, so did her convictions about her complications concerning sex-related emotional baggage. When asked what kept her from celibacy, she responded in a way that many of us do: failure of religious institutions to give real answers regarding sex and a fear of how to communicate that choice to a mate.

Still wanting her to give celibacy serious consideration, I asked her to speak about the role that sex has played in her life. In her own words she stated that, "Sex has played an important role in all of my relationships. It has been my voice in the majority of my relationships. It conveyed when I was happily connected to my mate or when I was disconnected from them." Yet like so many of us, her ideas of sex were misconstrued and led her to internalize this belief. Claire confessed that, "I grew up with a misconception that sex was a power tool for women in relationships. When your mate does something you don't like, you can withhold sex to kinda crack the whip and they'll tighten up!" While fortunately she's begun to realize that this is a poor mentality to have, how many of us still think this despite the overwhelming evidence to the contrary? Sex will never offer power and control over every aspect of your relationship and if you believe it will, you're setting yourself up for disappointment.

Often we continue to have difficulty in seeing how sex has affected our relationships and emotional self. Claire acknowledged that her sexual relationships tend to last no more than one year after sexual intimacy and that "when sex was removed, infidelity always followed." Because sex communicated emotion for Claire, her relationships never fully reached a level of true emotional intimacy that is built by real communication. Within her sexually intimate relationships, Claire says it has "made me feel a complete disconnect spiritually [and] masked a lot of ideologies that I should have dealt with years ago." Though Claire knew that spiritually, sex is a gift for marriage, she still chose to have sex when she "felt ready to move the relationship to the next level...EVERYTHING in my relationships has truly been driven by my emotions."

Digging a little deeper, however, her decisions to have sex were also driven by curiosity. When asked about the influence of those closest to her on her sexual decisions, she felt that she had no real conversations about sex with her natural family or her church family. Claire expressed that "the closest family to me don't have sex conversations. As much as it is taboo in the church, it's a magnified taboo in my family—even though my closest friends and I discuss sex regularly!" While she has witnessed relationship models of marriage, she says that "about 40% of them were unhealthy for the first 3-5 years and filled with massive power struggles, manipulation, and true lack of spiritual order," all of which are hallmarks of sexual relationships that lead to marriage but still carry with it the struggles related to the premature exchange of sexual energy.

Recently, Claire reunited with her high school sweetheart. The pair has had quite a storied history over the last decade that they've graced each other's lives. Unlike their previous romantic involvement, this reunion has not included sexual intimacy. In fact, when asked of their last intimate encounter, she detailed that it had been well over three years since their last act of physical intimacy. It is the first relationship where she's considering celibacy until marriage. When I asked her what role sex played in this relationship she expressed, "Sex was the be-all, end-all for our relationship. Our problems both revolved around and were masked by sex. Without sex, we both strayed from the relationship. So [sex] was the tie that binds." In the three years that they haven't had sex, however, she found that there had been a major transformation in the way they related to one another. When I asked her about this change, Claire explained, "The absence of sex has allowed us to see the person we are dealing with rather than the pleasure the person provides. For me, I've realized that he is the closest thing to perfect love that I've experience outside of the love I have for my children. He is the one man that I can sacrifice for in life because the sacrifice doesn't hurt. But I think the presence of sex before this clouded my ability to see this. With no sex, the clarity has shown me the storms we've weathered, the trials we've overcome, the levels where we both have matured and that ONLY GOD could give us this opportunity for a do over; A chance to perfect this seemingly perfect love (laughs)!"

Of course since they've historically had a sexual relationship, she now has to navigate the conversations of celibacy with partner. In preparing for this discussion with him she says, "I'm honestly not sure how he'll react. I think both of us are tired off bouncing back to each after having done so for 10 years, so I think he may actually be for it. In the couple of conversations that we had, sex doesn't hold a level of importance for him. He's more so performing out of the expectation of the females rather than true enjoyment." When I asked her to define how she sees their love beyond sex, her heart for her sweetie was readily apparent. Claire says that for her, 1 Corinthians 13:4-7 defines the two perfectly. She goes on to add, "Love, real love, is patient, kind, not boastful, or jealous. I feel all of those things about him. Although my heart would probably melt if we got married, I'm truly happy if he's with someone else and happy. His happiness is *so* very important to me with absolutely no expectation in return. Sex doesn't, and hasn't, allowed this love to manifest. It has previously made us jealous, easily angered, and place expectations where there should be none. Love beyond sex is joyfully and willingly experiencing the fullness of someone's presence with no self-fulfilling expectation."

Not surprisingly, she also has little encouragement from others with whom she's shared her consideration of celibacy. When asked about the reactions of others she shared, "When I mention it to people they either act as if they've seen a ghost or are completely puzzled. Many are like 'are you *really* considering that?' And this has been from older coworkers that attend the same church as I do as well as casual friends!" Strangely enough, she describes that these are the same kinds of people who criticize her for having two children out of wedlock. Since she is also a mother of two, I asked how she felt her celibacy would be perceived. "They may [question the celibacy decision]. Everyone has a right to feel how they choose, however, I'm at a point where I know what I need out of life! I know the legacy that I want to leave, the values that I want my children to hold, and the example I want to set for my daughter. I want her to know that though I may have started with the wrong beliefs about sex and its purpose, it's only a mistake if I choose not to address it before I take my last breath." As I've said before, your celibacy decision has to be done for you! People have opinions on everything that you do and if they desire, they will find a flaw in your actions good or bad.

While Claire has begun to recognize the issues that sex has brought to her life, including how unresolved emotional baggage affects her relationships with her children and family, she remains unconvinced fully that she can commit to celibacy. Like so many, she has questions of communicating her decision to a potential mate and how to successfully navigate a celibate relationship. She asks, "How do you remove the sexual frustrations from arguments and disagreements? How do you even do all of this without sounding like a crazed Christian?" All of which are relevant questions. If you are like Claire, I hope that those very questions have been answered as you read through this text. Maybe you've already chosen celibacy but still aren't sure what it's going to look like for you. To you I say: keep reading!

***

"I'm at the point where I want to do and be in His perfect will. Not because of anything He can do for me, but just because He is my God."
— Zaria, Miss Single & Celibate

Zaria, who recently ended a two-year relationship, has spent the last six months single and celibate. Her relationship ended mutually as the two could not come to an agreement on taking their relationship to the next level of marriage. Although this is not her first time being celibate, as she spent a year previously celibate before her last relationship, this is her first sustained commitment to celibacy until marriage. In this time of singleness, her spiritual walk has been incredibly strengthened and she's begun her own catharsis of self-awareness as a reward of her celibacy.

128

In her last relationship, Zaria stated that sex was not a direct issue or cause of the dissolution though she concedes that she felt she'd "given of myself and now I'm single." However, she does acknowledge the emotional relationship she has with sex. When asked to describe her relationship with sex she expressed, "Sex has caused emotional conflict in my life. Because I'm an emotional person, sex is an expression of love for me and has caused me to confuse sexual chemistry for emotional chemistry and love. When I have sex with a man, I expect a certain level of commitment, but did not get that [in my sexual relationships]." Like Claire, Zaria too saw sex as a tool of communication in relationships but Zaria's testimony will continue to show that this too can be overcome when you give your issues to God in full through the obedience of celibacy.

I asked Zaria what sparked her decision to become celibate. Her passion for her relationship with God overflowed, exclaiming "My decision to be celibate was made because I am at a point in my life where I desire to be as Christ-like as possible. Not just sexually, I am lining my life completely up with God and his commands. My entire life I have lived off of my intelligence and have expected for God to bless me because of this or that. I desire to be in the perfect will of God, not the permissive will of God. I therefore have to line my life up to the Word. In every aspect-physically, financially, sexually, mentally, emotionally- my goal is to be in the perfect will of God." This is the absolute attitude we must take when considering a commitment of celibacy. We often make plans and choices dependent on our ability but the commitment to celibacy is not, in my opinion, one of those. Making this choice invites the perfecting will of God in our lives and we must be prepared for all that comes with it.

When asked what revelations have come to her about her attitudes toward sex since her celibacy decision, she says "[I realized] that sex was not all that important, that it means so much more when you have a rue connection and know that God is in the midst of the relationship." More importantly, celibacy has given her the patience to wait on God's perfecting will in her life. She expressed that "whether one year or ten years from now, I'm looking forward to that connection with my soul mate, my husband." Her celibacy has not only allowed her to determine what role sex plays in her life, but it has also enlightened her of how her celibacy is best outfitted for her success. When asked of her feelings about masturbation as a safe sexual release for the celibate, she didn't believe that it was a sin but in her decision to be celibate she "chose to abstain from masturbation [as well]. I believe that it can get in the way of developing a closer relationship with God given that it can be a slippery slope." While my personal beliefs on celibacy and masturbation differ only slightly, Zaria's rationale for *her* best form of celibacy cannot be denied. She went on to say that, "I am choosing to be celibate so that I can focus on God as the center of my life, and I cannot afford to let **ANYTHING** get in the middle of that. In my moments of weakness, my goal is learn to focus on God solely so I believe it is totally possible to accomplish this." As always, you must decide how your celibacy best fits you within reason, of course! Are you like Zaria, whose heart is on fire for God and know that your walk will be strengthened in giving up sex? *Miss Single & Celibate* offers some powerful words of advice to those who are celibate and considering:

"In your decision to be celibate, you must first make the commitment to yourself and God. Like any vow, once you make the commitment to God He takes that vow seriously and expects for you not to break it. Once you make the vow, it is then yours to embrace, love, and keep. One thing to remember is to not let others try and make you feel like your decision is crazy or made with ill intent. Others may not feel like you cannot stick to it, but through Christ all things are possible. People, because of their self-righteousness, may also try and make you feel like your decision is for some other reason. But the great thing about it is that only God knows the heart of a man. Celibacy also has a way of giving you clear discernment about your life and the people you are surrounded by. It also gives you clarity on your purpose in life."

So what's it all for or what is the end goal, you may ask? How do all of these principles and ideas discussed so far in *Closed Legs Do Get Fed* play out in reality in relationships? If you stick with it and follow the will of God, it could blossom into a beautiful marriage that is nestled safely in the hand of God like the testimony of Kamille, *Mrs. Married from Celibacy.*

***

"I trusted God to bring me the desires of my heart as I continued to delight in Him; not compromising or settling for less than the expectation of a man after God's own heart. If he didn't love God, he wouldn't be able to love me."
– Kamille, *Mrs. Married from Celibacy*

Kamille, who recently tied the knot with her husband, enjoyed a celibate courtship with her now-husband for two years. The two, who made celibacy vows prior to meeting, made a conscious decision together to remain celibate until marriage in their relationship. For both, it was the first celibate relationship after their individual vows of celibacy in their adult years. For me, I've had the wonderful pleasure of watching Kamille grow from a babe in Christ into an ever-maturing disciple that brings other souls closer to the Kingdom. Kamille has served as a model, sounding board, and Godly counsel for me through her transparency in the path of her courtship into marriage. I hope that you are as encouraged by the testament of the fruits of the Godly obedience of her and her husband as I have been!

During our conversation, Kamille spent quite a bit of time defining love—and I didn't even have to ask her to do so! When I asked how her celibate relationship came to be, she explained that "we were both celibate before we met and in addition to our celibacy vows, we also vowed that the next person we dated—spent ample time with and opened our hearts to— would be our spouse...[When going into a relationship, I knew] loving me included respecting my celibacy and my relationship with God. Love is giving someone what is best for them and *there is nothing better than God*." Prior to meeting, Kamille waited patiently in her singleness for over a year while her husband had been waiting over *three* years in his own singleness! So many of us wonder what we should so if we meet someone who loves God but seems to be unwilling to commit to a celibate relationship with us. Should we lead by example? Should we walk away without giving it a chance? Kamille expresses that for her, "if any relationship was hurting my relationship with The Lord, then it was time to go. I can't walk with someone who is not heading in the same direction as me, who is not walking at the same pace as me, or who is trying to take different routes that God said I should not take." The fact that both she and her would-be-husband were both in love with God made it easier to put Him at the head and helm of their courtship.

Just as salvation doesn't automatically make many of us accept celibacy, you don't have to have to accept salvation to engage in celibacy. For believers, celibacy obviously has different tenets and connotations but it is well possible to be celibate without an Abrahamic (Judaism, Islam, and Christianity) or other religious faith. As Kamille explains, "I know there are some who are doing it [celibacy] without God but, in today's over-sexualized media, a relationship with God provides much needed peace of mind, self-control, focus, and most importantly, accountability." When describing how she personally came to her decision of celibacy, she revealed that it was one before she accepted salvation. Kamille further explains that she was "tired of the continuous cycle of giving up more and more of me and leaving with less of me than I began with. I knew it was time for a change, and celibacy seemed like the smartest thing I could do. I hoped it would teach me discernment. [I began to learn that] men are cunning and patient. When they want something bad enough, they will do just about anything to get it simply for the pride of the catch." While explaining what her discernment during celibacy exposed her to in relationships, she stated, "Time exposes all things, especially inconsistencies. If a man really wants my heart he will marry, if not he will give up. If He wants sex then He will marry, but during the time of waiting, his intentions would be exposed before I am deceived, especially when you pray to the God of truth. My eyes were opened to the true intentions of men, and I felt being celibate would weed out who really loved me." Giving her life to Christ only sharpened her self-awareness: "Upon getting saved, I realized I only have one body. I knew I was going to have to give an account of my history to God, if I continued to indulge in my flesh, and to my husband. I knew I would be putting myself at risk for diseases, I would probably lack trust for my husband, lose respect for myself, and the list goes on!"

So as the questions tend to go, when people learn that you are celibate or were before marrying they are dumbfounded that you were actually able to do it. When I asked how she and her husband decided to outfit their celibacy and determine their physical boundaries, she explained, "We tried the whole not kissing thing, several times (though I do recommend a no kissing policy). We once went about eight months without kissing, but we slipped up here and there, you know how you tend to get all googly eyed with each other from time to time (laughs)! However, we spent more time actually getting to know one another, getting to know each other's souls. Our relationship was long distance so this helped give us an environment where we could effectively do this." Contrary to popular belief, long distance relationships are not easier to keep celibate. If anything, the distance intensifies the desire to be physically affectionate with one another when you are physically together. Kamille describes how they handled their physical attraction while spending time together: "When we were able to physically spend time together, we did so in public places, and at family members' houses. This does not mean that temptation didn't rear its head. The more we got to know each other's hearts and souls, the harder it became to resist one another. It's not impossible but A LOT of prayer was needed." Additionally, they made other physical boundaries that best fit their celibacy. Kamille describes their convictions about sexual attitudes, expressing that, "We already had convictions about certain things that God prepared us for in His word, sex is more than physical; it deals with the heart. We were convinced that oral sex, masturbation, and fondling were just as bad as fornication; all these are products of lusting. I mean, in the end these things don't ever just stop there." Again, I emphasize that you must decide how your celibacy best looks for you and your relationship. Kamille's courtship involved practical ways of abstinence in that they spent more time learning one another on emotionally and spiritually intimate levels, serving as one another's accountability partner for maturity in Christ, not spending an overabundance of alone time together, and avoiding heavy kissing. When speaking on the difficulties of their celibacy outfit, she says "This was extremely hard but when you desire to do God's will, He will grace you for it. We had to constantly be reminded of His word. In the heat of the moment, the last thing on our minds was a scripture but it was in those moments that we depended on God's grace and the conviction He broke our hearts with if we had strong desires to do something sinful."

Contrary to held beliefs; celibacy doesn't make it more difficult to establish intimacy in a relationship. As Kamille reiterates, "Especially having God at the center...it was easier. Waiting for marriage helps to build MORE trust, intimacy, companionship, and romance, than not waiting. You really get to know a person for who they are and not what they can offer you. Sex tends to distract or blindfold the true person behind the sexual pleasure. There was a lot of genuineness and purity in our responses to each other's love. It makes you strive to find creative ways to show love for someone. It is a lie to believe that sex will develop love and emotional intimacy; sex in itself is just a means to fulfilling a desire and intimacy is separate from sex. It's a desire of its own, and it can and will be fulfilled whether there is sex or not. Intimacy is the desire to develop love, sex is the desire for... well, sex."

Celibacy also doesn't give us immunity to the normal struggles and disagreements we find in our romantic interpersonal relationships. Though Kamille didn't experience arguments about sex and found that their celibacy covenant actually sustained the courtship, she is not shy about acknowledging the existence of tension during their courtship. In a moment of candid transparency, Kamille shared that "Celibacy did not eliminate struggles in our relationship. To be honest, towards the end of our courtship, it probably made it harder as tensions rose from not being able to connect on that last level, physical intimacy. It's hard to stay celibate for years upon years when you truly love someone! At some point, you have to get married (laughs)! I, as a woman, still had to deal with issues from past relationships, as well as my husband's past...and my husband had to deal with my past as well. We argued A LOT, as we were moving toward becoming one flesh in other aspects aside from sex. The closer we got to each other's hearts, the easier it was to hurt each other. And we definitely suffered many hurts while, "learning," how to be in a relationship all over again, and doing it God's way. Not having sex gave us clearer vision to address them, to handle and settle them." She does offer invaluable advice for those of us who are in or are considering celibate relationships: "We are all crazy people with our own weird preferences and perspectives. Anytime you have two people together long enough, there will always be disputes and disagreements. This teaches you how to be patient and work through, them to overcome them in love and not just cover them up with sexual passion. The heart is so complex, and we needed God's help, prayer and His word to guide us through. Pushing God out of it would only make us coax or ignore what the real issues were. He knows our hearts, what we need and so on. Every problem we have is one we have because of not honoring Him by striving to be like Him."

When describing their road to engagement and marriage, Kamille revealed that they didn't put their relationship on a timeline although they knew from the foundation that they would get married. Like so many of us, Kamille and her then-boyfriend spent so much time waiting on life to offer them the perfect circumstances to wed that their months of courtship turned into a year and an indefinite possibility of those "perfect circumstances" ever appearing. At the 18-month mark, the pair finally began to create a timeline upon her partner's return from overseas. Though their perfect circumstances had yet to appear, she expressed that "These things have their place— finances, security, stability, etc.—but so does trusting God. It got to a point where we would have had to either put our love on pause, or just get married because our hearts were growing too close. Compromising our purity was not an option. We began to do bible studies, sought counsel from trusted spiritual authorities, and of course prayed about what God wanted. Love always gives you a choice." As the two sought the Word of God for direction, they learned that dating simply is not biblical; according to the bible we are betrothed, married, or unmarried. So biblically speaking, they learned that their period of dating and courtship was actually their engagement. Her husband would propose to her on a cold winter day and they would be married two *days* later in a beautiful courthouse nuptial. She feels that celibacy absolutely strengthened her marriage, going on to say "I seriously doubt we would be married if we had sex before getting married. I mean, what's the point of getting married if he has all the other benefits? Marriage then just becomes a title and loses its substance. Of course marriage is not all about sex but it is one of the pillars for it."

Kamille's testimony is a powerful example of what happens when we give over our permissive will to the perfecting will of God. She candidly expressed her celibacy in a way that is both transparent and relatable. Celibacy, at any stage of life, is simply not easy but it is an undertaking that is transformative and rewarding on more levels than sex itself. Sex only rewards us with an orgasm but celibacy rewards us reclamation of our sexual power, our spiritual sight, and a true awareness of whom we are and what we have to offer this world. Mrs. Married from Celibacy offers these words of wisdom to those who are celibate or considering celibacy: "Being celibate, and staying celibate, until marriage is not easy. Without God, it's probably close to impossible. Don't put yourself in situation where you know it will be hard for you to get out of. Know your limits and your boundaries, and don't be afraid to set some REALISTIC standards, such as... the person you date has a desire to be celibate as well. STAND for what you believe in! Celibacy is an investment into your future; the benefit that it gives outweighs the immediate and fleeting pleasure of sex outside of marriage. Use your time of celibacy and singleness to prepare for your spouse. Your body is a gift to your spouse; let them know how much you love them now, by waiting until you marry them before you, "give it to them." Let God know you love Him more by giving Him your desires now, because if you delight yourself in the Lord, He will give you the desires of your heart. And when you meet the one God has created for you, and you WILL know, don't delay on starting your lives together! My husband and I wasted too much time waiting for perfect circumstances, a desired income bracket and the American dream before we got married. We gave those up and just went for it, and we are both so happy we did! God is faithful! Stay pure, stay true to yourself and faithful to God. He works all things together for the good of those who love Him and who He has called according to His purposes. Oh, and by the way... He makes ALL THINGS NEW!"

***

The testimonies shared here don't even begin to scratch the surface of the thousands of stories like them. You probably have seen yourself in one or more of them because our experiences with sex and celibacy, although unique, share many commonalities. Celibacy, even with all of its trials and tribulations, offers a beautiful experience of self-love, self-awareness, and enlightenment. These testimonies are not here to sway your decision one way or the other. As with everything in this book, the words of these three women should give you cause to pause and reflect on your own life experiences that may parallel the ones detailed here. So as the word would say, *Selah*; think and meditate on the things that are written here.

Reflection Questions for Chapters 12-15

The following questions are presented for the sake of introspection and to guide discourse among couples and friends. You are welcome to continue reading the book without answering— no one is keeping score!

1. How many conversation areas have you and your mate covered as discussed in chapters 11 and 12? Do you feel satisfied with what you've learned or is there a need to revisit certain areas?

2. Do you feel that you've been able to keep the spark alive in your relationship in the absence of sex? If not, why and what will you do to improve this?

3. Would you and your partner considering living together during your engagement period? If not, what do you feel are the obstacles that you both cannot overcome?

4. Have you had any of the recommended conversations in Chapter 12 during your engagement period? Are you satisfied with the discussion or are there areas you will need to revisit?

5. If you've recently endured a breakup, have you learned in what ways you and your partner contributed to it?

6. If you're feeling angry with God about a recent breakup (or anything really), do you now feel better equipped to express

and deal with it in a positive way?

7. Can you identify and name the benefits of your past failed relationships? How have those lessons impacted your life currently?

8. Do you have a better understanding of God's plan in rejection?

9. Do you see yourself in Claire, Zaria, or Kamille? In what ways?

10. Do the testimonies of these women bring you comfort or clarity? In what ways?

16: PASSING THE TORCH OF KNOWLEDGE

Often when we are introduced to new knowledge we work hard to retain it and commit it to memory. The knowledge becomes our dogma, our cardinal and rigid rules by which we live our lives. The intent of the knowledge presented in this book is not for you to simply apply it to memory but to live the spirit of its intent. Though it is not possible for me to cover everything, it has been my goal to give you an honest reflection of celibacy. I have experienced the oppression of religious teachings that burdened me as a woman and shamed me for my sexual nature. In these pages, however, I hope that I've shown you that it is not necessary to make choices between your intellect, your heart, your spirit, your sexual nature, or your faith. These things are part of the whole and the neglect of one forsakes the health of the others.

I hope you walk away knowing how to treat the sexually created soul ties of your life, when you're truly ready to commit to celibacy, and what will accompany this decision. Not everyone will support or understand your choice, and that's okay. Celibacy is one of the most positively selfish choices we make that requires no apologies. We often get caught up in the belief that all selfishness is negative but Scholar Audre Lorde put it best: "Caring for myself is not self-indulgence, it is self-preservation and that is an act of political warfare." The choice to consider and pursue celibacy is an act of self-care. It is an act that says your experiences and feelings are valid and that you're worthy of positive emotional health free from the stress that premature sexual energy invites into our lives. Celibacy is an act of self-care that rejects the pressure to conform and restrict our sexual expression to the expectations of romantic partners and a collective social attitude that views celibacy negatively.

Your choice of sexual celibacy is not one meant to oppress your sexuality but to give you sexual agency. As women sex often becomes our means of giving and receiving everything except sexual pleasure in our relationships, leaving us empty if the relationship ends. This book seeks to send the message that we take control of our sexual selves not in an effort to please men but to please ourselves in addition to pleasing God. Taking control of our sexual selves through celibacy should allow us the opportunity to say simply "I am enough" when deciding what we have to offer in relationships.

Though you've learned that celibacy is difficult and requires constant work, I also hope that you have been enlightened to its true rewards and the fruit it will bear in your life. It *is* possible to find happiness in celibacy regardless to where you are in your life's journey. Celibacy isn't designed to be a burden but to lift the burdens that have been added to your life through past experiences of sexual intimacy. Committing to

145

this life choice will test and break you but only to free and heal you from all of the emotional and spiritual baggage you've picked up along the way.

Women, you're not worthless because you've had sex once or a thousand times. You have only devalued yourself if you haven't taken the time to emotionally heal from all of the things heaped on you through your exchanges of sexual energy. Celibacy is not a choice you should feel pressured to make in hopes of redeeming yourself as "good woman" in the eyes of anyone. In all the things that Proverbs 31 describes as a virtuous woman, not one of them requires that her sexual past is pleasing to the view of society. A virtuous woman is one whose inner beauty comes only through Christ and seeks God with her entire being in order to align her life to His will. Yes, you will have to account to your mate and to God for the sexual past. If your mate doesn't recognize what a virtuous woman is and that in Christ you've become a new creature, don't subject yourself to the emotional trauma. Celibacy does not produce guilt that we should hold on to for life. It produces deliverance and unquestioned forgiveness from God and best believe that your romantic relationships should do just the same.

Finally, I hope that you will never approach your conversation of celibacy the same. I hope that you never think of your sexual nature as taboo and incompatible with your faith. If we are to believe that God made everything, it cannot exclude the things that make us uncomfortable—including human sexuality! Openly embracing

146

your sexuality with honesty and positive sexual attitudes is perhaps the most paramount decision you will make in your commitment to celibacy.

As our conversation comes to a close, I continue to echo my opening sentiments. You still may not choose a life of celibacy, at least not this day or hour. Certainly, however, I hope the words that have been written here are seeds of knowledge that will take root, grow, and bear fruit through you passing this knowledge along to others.

Thank you.

Discussion Questions for *Closed Legs Do Get Fed*

1. Having finished the book, what are your feelings concerning celibacy, sex, and faith now? Do you feel more comfortable with the balance of these things?

2. What new discoveries have you made about yourself or your partner while reading? What will you do with these new recognitions?

3. (For Women) Do you feel more empowered and comfortable with your sexual nature?

4. Do you have a better understanding about the spiritual and emotional components of sex?

5. What things do you strongly agree or disagree about within the book?

6. Do you now feel encouraged to begin or continue a celibacy covenant?

7. What shocked or surprised you most about this book? Have you ever had a conversation this open and honest about the challenges and rewards of celibacy before?

8. Do you believe your life and/or relationship will improve given the knowledge you have gained? If so, how?

9. What are the top three things you will take away from this book?

REACH OUT AND TOUCH SOMEONE

No one, not even people of faith, are exempt from emotional turmoil. When your prayer is finished, sometimes the answer is to talk to a professional who is capable of partnering with you on your path to emotional health. If you're going through a challenge that you feel is more than you can bear, do not be afraid or ashamed to reach out for help. Below are a few helpful support sources. Please, if you need them, use them.

DEPRESSION HOTLINE: (630) 482-9696
Depression is real and more common than we tend to believe. It's more than feeling "a little blue" and it's not a result of evil spirits. It comes as a result of our personality structure, hormonal chemistry and emotional patterns. If you're feeling worthless, sleepless, sadness, guilt, or persistent feelings of emptiness and need to talk it out with someone, please use the number above.

EATING DISORDERS HOTLINE: (847) 831-3438
If you or someone you know is struggling with anorexia, bulimia, disordered eating, or other eating disorders and wants to get help, please call the number above.

EXHALE [AFTER ABORTION SUPPORT]: (866) 439-4253
Do you need to talk to someone about your personal abortion experience without

condemnation? Exhale provides free emotional support, resources, and information to women who've had abortions and their partners, friends, and family.

GRIEF SUPPORT: (650) 321-5272
You don't have to grieve your losses alone. If you're overwhelmed by the grief of a recent loss, please call the number above for support.

LIFELINE SUICIDE PREVENTION: (800) 273-8255
If you or someone you know is experiencing persistent thoughts of suicide, please call and talk to someone who can help.

RAPE AND SEXUAL ASSAULT: (800) 656-4673
Rape and sexual assault are **never okay and it is never your fault.** If you've been a victim, in crisis, or are in need of support, please call the number above.

GLBT YOUTH TALKLINE [SEXUALITY SUPPORT]: (800) 246-7743
The GLBT Youth Talkline is here to help those 25 and under discuss issues concerning coming-out, relationship issues unique to the LGBTQIQ community, family and school conflicts, and safer-sex support.

TREVOR PROJECT: (866) 488-7386
Are you an LGBTQ person who is struggling with thoughts of suicide, in crisis, or need a safe-space to talk? The Trevor Lifeline is here for your support at the number above.

ABOUT THE AUTHOR

Making her debut with Closed Legs Do Get Fed, D. Danyelle is a woman who is passionate about both women's sexual agency and the reconciliation of sexuality and faith. Tallahassee made and Atlanta matured, she's previously written both as an academic and copywriter. When she is not working as an author, she serves as a Public Policy professional and a freelance web and graphic designer for Urbanizd Skillz Design Suite. She is an alumnus of Georgia State University where she earned both her Bachelor of Arts in African American Studies and Master of Public Policy, Social Policy.

Thank you again for reading! Your thoughts, feelings, and opinions are valuable to and for me!

Reviews from other unbiased readers encourage others to try this book as well! In addition to your real life discussions with friends about this book, please don't forget to review it on Amazon or your place of purchase or feel free to leave a comment on Facebook at facebook.com/ClosedLegsDoGetFed.

If you would like to reach out to me personally with your testimony or even your hate mail (smiles), feel free to email closedlegsdogetfed@gmail.com

Works Cited:

Ann Kiki Anaebere, Adeline Nyamathi, Sally
Maliski, Chandra Ford, Angela Hudson,
and Deborah Koniak-Griffin. She Decides:
Sex Partner Selection Decision Making and
African American Women. Journal of Black
Studies November 2012 43: 872-892, first
published on September 12, 2012
doi:10.1177/0021934712459958

Burgest, D.R. (1990). Sexual games in Black
male/female relations. *Journal of Black
Studies, 21*(1), 103-116.

Credit Karma http://www.creditkarma.com

Drake, ST. C. and H. Cayton (1945) Black
Metropolis. New York: Schocken. Frazier,
E. F. (1974) The Negro Church in America.
New York: Schoken. Nelsen, H. M. and
Nelsen A.K. (1975) Black Church in the
Sixties. Lexington: Univ. Press of Kentucky.

Gallup Report (1984) Religion in America.

Gonzales, A.M., & Rolison, G. (2005). Social
oppression and attitudes toward sexual
practices. Journal of Black Studies, 35(6),
715-729.

Teachman, J. (2003), Premarital Sex, Premarital
Cohabitation, and the Risk of Subsequent
Marital Dissolution Among Women.

Journal of Marriage and Family, 65: 444–455. doi: 10.1111/j.1741-3737.2003.00444.x

U.S. Department of Health and Human Services, National Institutes of Health. (2013). *HIV hides from the immune system*. Retrieved from National Institutes of Health website: http://www.niaid.nih.gov/topics/HIVAIDS/Understanding/Biology/pages/hidesimmunesystem.aspx

All interviews conducted, transcribed, and edited by the author of this work. All interview quotes were used and edited with permission from interview participants. The views expressed in this work do not necessarily reflect the personal views of these participants.

Thank you for reading this work, we certainly hope you have enjoyed it. We hope you will pick up other offerings from this Author in the future.

Here are other offerings currently available from the Kirabaco Publishing Catalog:

Author KR Bankston Presents (Fiction):

- ***The Gianni Legacy (in order) Ebook and Paperback***
- A Deadly Encounter, Sins of the Father, Smoke & Mirrors, Life After Death

- ***Thin Ice the Serial Novel Series: (ebook only)***
- Thin Ice , Thin Ice 2 – Hide & Seek, Thin Ice 3 – Armageddon, Thin Ice 4 – Resurrections, Thin Ice 5 – Checkmate, Thin Ice 6 – Hangman & Socrates, Thin Ice 7 – Echoes of Reckoning, Thin Ice 8 – Separazione Finale, Thin Ice 9 – Epiphany Thin Ice 10 – Ambition Thin Ice 11 – Homecomings Thin Ice 12 – Siren Song

- **Stand Alone Titles**
- King of the Game, The Master Orchestrator, Now You're A Star, Crossroads: An Anthology ,Three The Hard Way

TURN THE PAGE

Liberation is not a gift bestowed upon us from our oppressor.
It is taken and owned by the decision that NO ONE can keep them from it.

For too long we've watched silently as we've been violated by our government at every turn. The rights and needs of the poor, minorities, and women have been ignored and trampled upon. It's time to stand up and say no. You have the power to make a difference and it is as simple as casting a ballot in your local, state, and federal elections.

If you haven't registered to vote, you may do so in the following ways:
- Contact your Secretary of State and request a voter registration form by mail
- Register at your Public Library
- Register at the DMV when you renew your license
- Register when you renew your TANF/Food Stamp benefits

Registering to vote doesn't automatically sentence you to jury duty. If you get a jury summons, don't avoid it! We need rational voices to keep our men and women from behind bars! **Convicted felons are not barred from registering!** States such as Rhode Island, South Carolina and Utah automatically restore your voting rights upon completion of your sentence. Check your state laws for complete information on restoring your voting rights if you've been convicted of a felony.

To Report Voter Issues: call the Civil Rights Division toll-free at <u>(800) 253-3931</u>, or contact them by mail at:
Chief, Voting Section
Civil Rights Division Room 7254 - NWB
Department of Justice
950 Pennsylvania Ave., N.W.
Washington, DC 20530

Your right to vote was secured through blood, sweat, and tears. Exercise it to the fullest without relenting. Social change and justice for people of color is not optional: it is mandatory. Make them know this by registering your voting voice today!

CPSIA information can be obtained at www.ICGtesting.com
Printed in the USA
BVOW04s2051290714

360928BV00029B/477/P